*Inspiration
for
Embroidery*

Inspiration for Embroidery

Constance Howard

B T BATSFORD LTD
LONDON

By the same author

Embroidery and Colour 1976
Twentieth Century Embroidery in Great Britain to 1939 1981
Twentieth Century Embroidery in Great Britain from 1940 to 1963 1983
Twentieth Century Embroidery in Great Britain from 1964 to 1977 1984
Constance Howard Book of Stitches 1979

ISBN 0 7134 4768 0

First published 1966

Second edition 1967

Reprinted 1967, 1968, 1970, 1971, 1973, 1976

First published in paperback 1985

Cover illustration: detail from an embroidery by Constance Howard

Printed & bound in Great Britain by Anchor Brendon Ltd, Tiptree, Essex
for the publishers
B T Batsford Ltd, 4 Fitzhardinge Street, London W1H 0AH

Contents

Acknowledgment

I would like to thank Ann and Michael Preston for their interest and for providing me with a week-end of peace and quiet, during which time I revised my ideas and decided to continue my half finished manuscript, but from a fresh point of view. Without their encouragement this book would not have been completed.

My very grateful thanks are also due to Molly Picken who composed and drew the majority of the illustrations; to Julie Dorrington who photographed most of the examples of embroidery with the help of her parents who fetched and returned work at any time, often at short notice, and always cheerfully; to all the staff and past and present students in the embroidery department of The School of Art, Goldsmiths College and other colleges of education, who loaned work and provided a great number of examples of embroidery which have given the main interest to the book, and without whose co-operation the book could not have been produced.

I would like to thank the Administrations of the British Museum and of the Victoria and Albert Museum for allowing drawings to be made from their collections, also the staff of B. T. Batsford Limited, who have had the patience of Job in waiting for the manuscript which was long overdue, and for their more than co-operative help on all occasions.

Chiswick 1966   C.H.

Introduction

The popularity of embroidery has increased during recent years, and with this a higher standard of design and workmanship has developed, but there is still much scope for the encouragement of originality in ideas and the ways and means by which design and pattern making may be understood more fully. Technical skill is only a part of any craft, without which progress is limited, but 'how to make something', without building up aesthetic appreciation and a sensibility in taste, is worthless. The two are inseparable in embroidery if good results are to be achieved. Previously this aspect of the craft was not pursued to the same standard as that of technical achievement, and was considered of lesser value than the skill to work perfect stitchery. This lack of interest in design and subsequent inability to appreciate its importance may be due to the fact that much of the technique of embroidery is still very similar to that of the sixteenth century or earlier. Most of the stitches used nowadays have been handed down, generation by generation with little variation, whereas styles of design have changed considerably especially during this century; therefore, unless there is a sound basis on which to start building up patterns, it is much harder to keep abreast of the varying approaches to art now prevalent, than to practise stitchery which shows little apparent change. It is a waste of time to put good workmanship into articles of inferior design and made of poor quality materials.

It is a fallacy to think that original design can only be achieved after years of training. With an open mind and unbiased thought a great deal may be attempted from the outset.

The embroidering of simple but original designs should give more satisfaction than the working of commercial transfers, however elaborate: with this approach the craft becomes doubly exciting, the interpretation of these patterns becomes an adventure and the result an individual creation.

Tradition is admirable but ideas should be adjusted to the present day, with embroidery in keeping with the period, rather than relying on the past for inspiration and technique. This book has been compiled for the embroiderer who has a good working knowledge of stitchery but who may have had little or no practice in designing. There is sufficient information and instruction here to encourage the building up of original ideas from the simple basic structure to the more complicated, finished design.

Embroidery has been chosen, when possible, without 'stylization' in order that it may not date too quickly, although it is difficult to avoid most craftwork as being recognizable of a particular period; however, this gives it is special character and should not be disparaged. Embroidery being linked particularly with interior decoration, woven and printed textiles and dress cannot escape the influences of current trends and the rapidly changing whims and fancies of fashion. If it is sound basically in design and workmanship, it should outlive the superficial qualities and so-called 'novelties' of an era.

It is hoped that the illustrations will spark off ideas and encourage experiment by those who have technical ability but who have not dared to escape from tradition, either in trying to design or in attempting to use stitchery in an unorthodox manner. Without a willingness to experiment with embroidery in all its aspects, that is with design, materials, threads and techniques, the full potentialities of a very exciting medium can never be realized. Embroidery is a slow process and the aim here is to give suggestions for study and experiment, not recipes for quick results, so that original thought is not cramped but extended. Ideas mentioned are the beginning of creative embroidery from which the individual approach develops and if patience and perseverance are maintained, together with a very simple attitude to design at the beginning, it should be possible to reach an advanced level. Time does not enter into this. Some people will grasp ideas quickly, others more slowly; it does not matter so long as each stage of progress is understood before attempting a more difficult one. Success also depends on the amount of time given to study and research as no progress can be made without these. The same may be said of any skill in which the mastering of certain techniques must accompany artistic sensibility; they are inter-related and cannot be skimped, nor thought of separately.

Background Appreciation

Embroidery is one of the most exciting and satisfying crafts of today. There is nothing to prevent it from increasing in popularity, as it is one most easily practised in the home; it requires the minimum of bulky equipment and it need not take up a great deal of space, although this is a debatable point for embroidered hangings may be of a considerable size, and the collecting of pieces of fabric for patchwork and appliqué can become a mania, filling every available drawer and cupboard!

Embroidery developed to a really high standard of design and craftsmanship is inimitable, and can be classed with fine art if approached from an intellectual creative level. On the other hand it can sink to the lowest form of crudity both in design and workmanship. This lack of quality so often apparent, has fostered the idea that embroidery has little or no artistic merit, and in fact is thought of as a 'homecraft' or a hobby and dismissed as such.

Although good embroidery is appreciated there is still too little of it to be seen, and it is hoped that with a raising of standards of design more people will begin to realize its possibilities for the decoration of public buildings, the home and for dress, in the secular as well as in the ecclesiastical field. There is a heritage of superb English embroidery, the tradition of which began during the Middle Ages when embroidery for church vestments and hangings was carried out by the nuns in convents and by professional guilds of broiderers, the designs often being adapted from illuminated manuscripts of the period. During the thirteenth and fourteenth centuries this work became famed throughout the civilized world, both for its superior quality in design and excellence of workmanship. It was known as *Opus Anglicanum* and superbly embroidered vestments were exported to various European capitals, where some of them are still to be seen in museums and churches; there are also excellent examples in the Victoria and Albert Museum, London. The Black Death of 1348 killed many skilled workers and with the dissolution of the monasteries much ecclesiastical work was destroyed or cut up for domestic articles; church embroidery tended to deteriorate and disappear, but an interest in embroidery for costume and furnishings developed. During the sixteenth and seventeenth centuries domestic embroidery flourished, producing a richness and exuberance, and an individuality of style which became recognized as typically English, in spite of the many foreign influences prevalent at that time. Until the eighteenth century embroidery was a part of the occupation of the average English household, being employed originally as a necessity for patching, darning and sewing seams, and also as a means of decorating plain fabrics to give them quality and interest. By the eighteenth century, however, embroidery was very costly, was professionally done, becoming a luxury for the rich only. Woven patterned silks and printed cottons obviated the necessity for other kinds of patterns and with the advent of embroidery machines during the nineteenth century, much hand embroidery on costume died out and by the end of the century was almost non-existent, as cheaper methods of decoration had been devised.

This was the position at the beginning of the twentieth century, in spite of the efforts of William Morris and his followers, who tried hard during the latter part of the nineteenth century to revive an interest in handicraft for its own sake in opposition to the machine-made article. Although some interesting ecclesiastical embroidery was designed by him and some architects, which was very good of its kind, his attempt had little apparent success in this country, although his influence had repercussions in Sweden, where it fostered a new interest in hand embroidery, mainly based on traditional design. This spread throughout the Scandinavian countries, then to Germany and eventually to Great Britain, which owed much of its contemporary style in the '50s to the Nordic traditional work.

During the Edwardian era, machine-manufactured Nottingham lace became so popular that household articles and clothes were trimmed lavishly with it, embroidery was superfluous, and although a few pioneers such as Mrs Archibald Christie and Lewis F. Day wrote excellent books on the subject and encouraged it in every way, embroidery became an almost dead craft. It was not until the 1920s that interest was revived, mainly in the schools of art, by Mrs Rebecca Crompton, who taught and was a considerable artist herself, working large panels in which hand and machine embroidery were often combined. This encouraged an interest in appliqué wall decorations, a fashion which has increased in popularity particularly during the post-war period when small pieces of various fabrics could be used to advantage for designs, without great cost.

Machine embroidery for the decoration of dress and household linens developed, the finer machine work helping to counteract the heavy 'arty' hand embroidery which was popular, but never smart nor suitable for the *haute couture* trade.

The Needlework Development Scheme was founded in 1934 in Scotland to help to raise the standards of embroidery design and needlework in its own schools. After the Second World War this scheme was extended to schools all over Great Britain and contributed considerably towards raising the general standard in the secondary modern, grammar and art schools throughout the country. By sending loan collections of good examples of embroideries round the schools and by publishing booklets and leaflets periodically, ideas and taste were developed which should have lasting effects on the children and lead to a better appreciation of embroidery as a craft both useful and decorative. Unfortunately this scheme is now disbanded.

During the war the production of new materials was curtailed, all fabrics became scarce, but embroidery flourished almost in spite of itself. Household goods and clothes were devoid of decoration and reduced to the purely utilitarian, so the need to relieve the monotony was partly satisfied by working patterns in any threads available, on any materials which could be collected. The creation of whole garments from scraps of odd materials, sewn together with decorative stitchery, became a great accomplishment. The idea of creating something from nothing was an added stimulus, as with the coupon system of rationing only small supplies of new materials could be obtained. Make-do-and-mend classes flourished throughout the country and were usually filled to capacity, for besides making useful renovations there was the pleasure of creating articles with colour and pattern in them. Great ingenuity was shown in using anything that came to hand both in threads and materials. The fact that there were difficulties in obtaining many of them made all the processes more exciting, as had there been a plentiful supply of materials available, interest might have waned and inventiveness died.

Fortunately that interest has been maintained and since the war there have been great advances in the manufacture of new materials of every kind. Those made from natural fibres are more satisfactory for embroidery as they have greater resilience, although it is a matter of experimenting with others made from synthetic yarns in order to find out which are most sympathetic in handling. Threads of various kinds are available, although some of the pure silk ones have not been manufactured since the war, owing to the high cost of production and others have now been discontinued. Various metal threads, real and synthetic, all kinds of beads, sequins and jewels now give almost too wide a field in which to experiment. It is rather a matter of limiting the choice in order to produce good embroidery, to avoid the danger of over-enthusiasm in using too many different kinds of threads and textures in one piece of work.

Embroidery is being done by students in schools of art in different parts of the country, where experiments in design and fabrics are helping to develop ideas and to give a wider knowledge of materials and various techniques, for dress, interior decoration and ecclesiastical work. Evening institutes, townswomen's guilds and women's institutes have flourishing embroidery classes but the emphasis often tends to be on technique, in which the appreciation of design and colour is sometimes lacking. This is due to the difficulty of getting teachers with both a design and technical training; on the other hand many classes have produced excellent original and experimental work, well carried out and lively in idea. Interest is increasing year by year which is encouraging,

and the appreciation of basic design, as a fundamental quality of good craftwork is there but needs guidance and stimulus to bring it out. The Embroiderers' Guild is supplying folios of historic and contemporary embroidery, information and leaflets to schools and institutes who belong to the Guild. It has an excellent library and is trying to improve its facilities and standards, all the time, so widening its membership and spreading information on all aspects of the craft.

Embroidery using the domestic sewing machine is becoming increasingly popular, as it is hard-wearing and particularly suitable for the decoration of clothes and household articles which require constant laundering. It is often less tedious to accomplish than some hand embroidery, and simple but effective patterns may be done in a short time, repetitive ones being more suitably worked by machine than by hand. There is, however, still prejudice against machine embroidery by those purists who do not believe in mechanical methods, and it is difficult to persuade them that there is any virtue whatever in the use of the machine, however good the results may be.

It would be encouraging to think that a national and characteristic style in English embroidery is developing, but this is difficult to determine, except in retrospect, as design is becoming increasingly international in outlook thus obscuring the country of origin of much of the 'non-peasant' craftwork of today. It might be suggested that the British flora and fauna are always an excellent basis from which to create designs, and that these designs might gradually inculcate a robust and recognizably British style, as distinct from a European one.

Sources of Inspiration

'What shall I do, I haven't any ideas?' This is often the answer when confronted with the prospect of designing. It is untrue, as everyone has ideas it the trouble is taken to clarify them. The imagined difficulties in the beginning that to create original design is impossible without a great deal of training may be 'off putting'. Perhaps little serious thought has been given to the question 'how does an idea start?'. There must be some point of departure; a beginning is to develop an awareness of the visual background, so that looking with purpose and intent becomes second nature. This kind of observation takes some time to perfect and entails concentrated and conscious effort but with this increased awareness, familiar surroundings take on new meaning and interest. To begin to see in this way, periods or days should be planned when there is time to look properly as this searching cannot be carried out in a few odd minutes. One period could be spent profitably looking for circular shapes or triangular shapes such as wheels, wrought iron scrolls, steeples, gabled roofs, chimneys and many other similar forms; another in searching for patterns or surface qualities on these same circular or triangular shapes either indoors or out. This could be followed by a day during which colour might be considered, notes being made on the great variety of reds or greens or any other colours

that can be discovered and where they are to be found, perhaps on an afternoon or morning walk; the rest of the day being spent in looking for similar colours indoors. These are only suggestions leading eventually to the exploration of form and colour at greater depth. If a note book is kept in which all the observations are recorded they are a beginning, from which ideas grow. From these notes and sketches it is much more satisfactory to make original designs which are an expression of the designer's personality and which are interpreted more to suit a particular purpose, than to take second-hand ideas and hope that they will prove suitable for the project in mind.

This is also why it is more valuable to study from reality than from photographs or reproductions as they are of someone else's point of view and show only one aspect of an object or natural form and not necessarily the best one. It is easier to remember things seen in actuality, as to examine them from all angles and to touch them if possible gives a better understanding of their constructions. Notes and sketches may be made from them, colour and texture more clearly seen and unusual views suggest exciting ideas for translation to design which could not have been observed from photographs. On the other hand photographs in newspapers and magazines are often excellent if first-hand information is unobtainable, they

2 Patterns made by tiling on roofs, where the repetition of a unit gives an all over texture

3 Tudor chimneys at Hampton Court on which patterns for patchwork, appliqué and quilting may be based

1 Wheels as a basis of pattern. These have many interpretations

4 Quilting based on patterns taken from the Hampton Court chimneys

suggest ideas sometimes unrelated to the forms shown in them. They should not be regarded as a substitute for reality, rather as a supplement to it.

A designer should aim at a deliberate and individual approach in carrying out an idea for a particular purpose, no two designers' results being the same even if the basic ideas are taken from a similar source. As information is collected and assimilated, critical and selective powers become more acute and it is easier to sift material of value from that to be discarded. As observation becomes sharpened so discrimination increases. By analysing shapes rather than details, by seeing the whole rather than the part, a simplicity of approach is developed so that basic forms and essential structures are understood better, details assume their proper importance and those with significant character may be included in the sketches and final patterns, those which do not help the complete idea being omitted.

Ideas may be stimulated in many other ways. One of the most important when designing is to commence with the materials without which no embroidery can be carried out. A rag bag is a source of excitement and inspiration in itself and the conglomeration of fabrics, textures and colours suggest ideas for their uses almost unconsciously. If excitement is not felt on looking at and handling fabrics, embroidery is not the craft to pursue. The textures of these fabrics are numerous. They may be woven so that the threads are counted easily and stitch patterns may be built up in this way on them or threads may be withdrawn to give open textures, those left being tied together with similar or contrasting colours, threads may be darned into nets making solid

6 Cut work and satin stitch, an idea from wheels

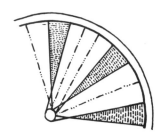

7 Shadow work or appliqué, based on the bicycle wheel

5 Quilting based on an idea evolved from wrought iron

8 Details from tyre treads, suitable for borders, in appliqué or outline embroidery

9 Threads withdrawn from hessian on the weft only, the remaining warp threads being tied together with weaving gimps, slubs and soft embroidery cottons to give interesting textures   *Goldsmiths*

patterns; in fact the basic structures of the original fabrics can be altered in a number of ways by patterns worked into them or printed on them, with stitchery added to increase the richness of effect. By experimenting with the variety of ways in which checked or striped fabrics may be used or in the choice and placing of stitchery when embroidering spots, many of the difficulties of planning are overcome in the critical early stages of design. Stitch patterns can be built up into borders or spots, using different thicknesses of

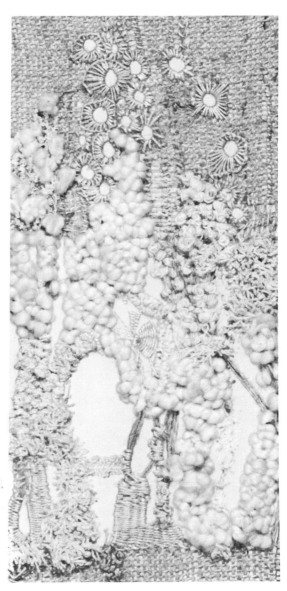

10 Experiment on hessian with threads withdrawn one way of the fabric; those remaining are tied together with heavy threads to give a variety of open shapes. Eyelets and french knots help to emphasize a chunky effect   *Judith Summers*

thread, the planning being in the choice of these threads, the closeness or openness of stitchery and the ability to use it creatively. Materials often suggest methods of work, technique may suggest

17

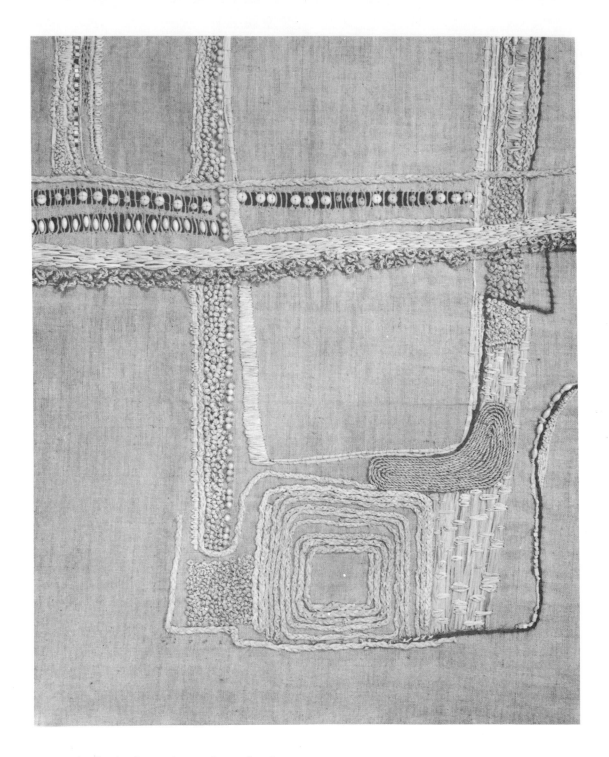

*11 Details of embroidery on hessian from a frontal, using
raffias, string, metal strips and wooden beads*
                    Susan Hathaway

12 A panel on hessian with buttons, kid and rug wool.
Here the materials have influenced the design
Christine Risley

limitations in design. Thick, heavy fabrics such as hessian, knobbly woollens, and some furnishing fabrics suggest coarse stitchery and bold pattern, sometimes using threads unravelled from them and incorporated as self coloured texture. Rug wools, gimps and slub weaving threads, string and knitting yarns may be used successfully with these backgrounds. Sometimes several techniques may be combined on one background fabric, pulled or drawn thread work with surface stitchery, shadow work and openwork or fine metal-thread embroidery with beads and jewels. This approach is interesting if the combination of techniques is unusual although at the same time they must look well together. Applied decoration using beads, sequins, leather, metal, buttons, even small stones, cords, ribbons, braids and fringes, in which the patterns are evolved from the arrangements of appliqué materials, can be exciting as long as the designer is not carried away by the profusion and diversity of the collection of bits and pieces, as they cannot all be applied to the same piece of work successfully without a hotchpotch result. Colour and texture of fabric often suggest ideas, some obvious such as brilliant, shiny blue or green silk or velvet for the beginning of a peacock or a fish, or an abstract pattern, derived from the study of water or movement of waves. Knobbly cream material could suggest stones and pebbles, while thin crisp material such as natural coloured silk taffeta might call to mind the brittle nature and dried colour of seed pods, grasses and leaves. Ideas multiply when thinking in these terms and whether the design is evolved first of all and the materials are chosen to suit it, or whether materials are to hand from which the pattern grows, does not matter, they and the threads are the basis of all embroidery and without a wide knowledge of these and their qualities, good embroidery cannot be accomplished. As progress is made it will be realized that the best materials should be chosen as it is a waste of time working on inferior ones. If cost is a major consideration, it is better to use a good quality cotton than a cheap imitation silk taffeta as a background and to embroider in threads suitable to this fabric.

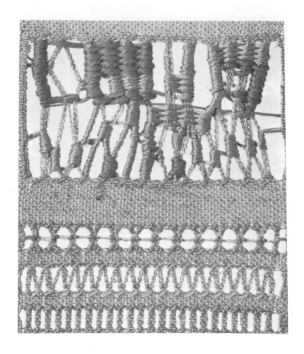

13 Simple drawn thread borders, and an attempt at a more enterprising result. This one has too many spaces of equal size and gives monotony instead of variety, and an unbalance with the heavy weaving

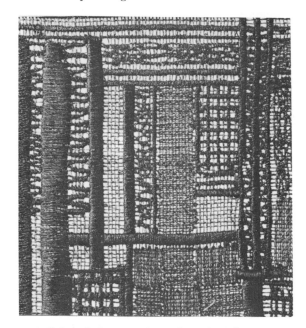

14 Pulled work done entirely on the Irish machine
Lydia Newman

15 A hand-printed pattern, embellished with machine embroidery

16 Two table mats from a set of six. The decoration is obtained by folding, pleating and cutting the gingham on the cross. Stitchery is not introduced   Judith Porritt Rachel McMillan College of Education

Purpose The idea is often born from the purpose of the article, involving the appropriate choice of fabric and a possible limitation in shape. In designing the embroidery for a cushion cover the kind of room and the décor in which the cushion is to be placed is of first consideration, both colour and texture and the style of decoration being planned to suit this background. The cover may be rectangular to conceal a pillow on a divan, the pattern designed with a right and a wrong way, or it could be square or circular, to be viewed from any angle, in which case the pattern should be planned with this consideration in mind. The shape may be asymmetrical, but whatever purpose the cushion plays in the room, this must be remembered in working out any ideas.

Embroidery may be needed to decorate a garment and in designing for this article a number of points must be taken into account which may limit the method of working and the way in which the ideas are developed. The garment may be for an adult; it may be for a child; it may have to be laundered or cleaned and if for an adult could be for day or evening wear, to be worn in daylight or artificial light. Fabric will be chosen according to these factors, therefore decoration must be appropriate. The shape of the garment will be determined by its purpose and from that the amount and distribution of the embroidery.

17 A cushion cover in black and white gingham, pleated, and threaded with black and white tapes. The nature of the fabric is quite changed from its original pattern. Embroidery could be added to give even greater change   Carla Crimble Rachel McMillan College of Education

These limitations sometimes make it easier to design as certain ideas are obviously unsuitable and must be rejected, the narrower scope of those suitable being played around with until satisfactory decoration is evolved.

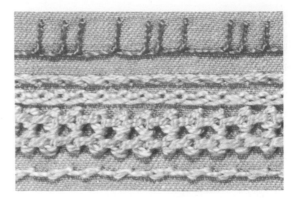

18 Stripes cut on the cross to form a chevron border, with simple stitchery added

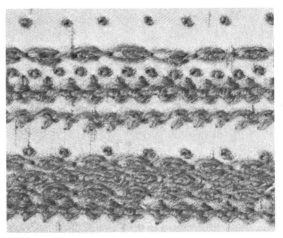

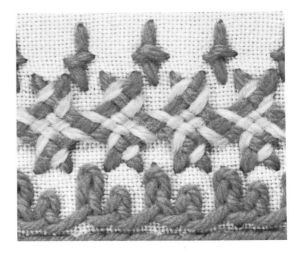

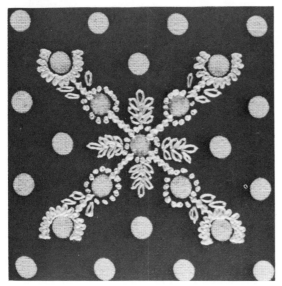

19 The letter X built up with stitches on a regularly printed spot-patterned fabric   *Eirian Short*

20 Three pattern borders built up entirely in stitchery
A border of thin lines and thick stitchery in perle
A border in wools
A border in very thick wools

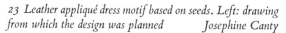

22 An experiment worked on Swedish curtain fabric, with the warp stripes woven openly and closely alternately. Drawn fabric and drawn thread stitchery, surface stitchery, wooden beads and bone curtain rings are intermingled. The whole is in colours of cream and white, with natural wooden beads in a variety of shapes   Sister Marie Louie

21 An experiment using a variety of threads, metal shapes and drawnthread work, on hessian   Goldsmiths

23 Leather appliqué dress motif based on seeds. Left: drawing from which the design was planned   Josephine Canty

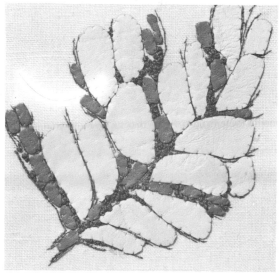

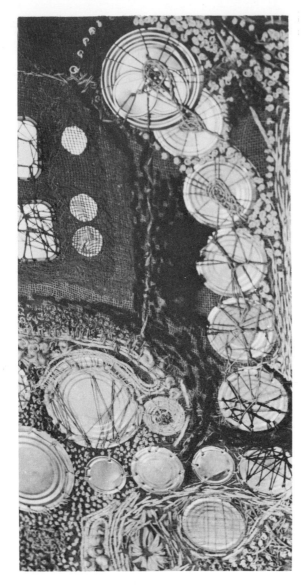

25 A decoration built up from seeds and pods, nuts and seed heads. The skilful arrangement of forms gives a good tonal balance to an interesting experiment *Marion Badley Trent Park College of Education*

24 A detail from a large hanging consisting of 'scrap' materials. Everything 'found' is used, the idea being based on the Indian mirror glass embroidery (shisha) with tin lids of all shapes and sizes substituted for glass in this large-scale decoration. Orange and carrot bags, string, raffia, sacking and anything available is incorporated if at all appropriate. The background is dyed hessian *Edward Holloway*

26 Part of the embroidery on a chasuble, showing a design based on cellular structure; worked entirely in pearl beads of different sizes, gold cords, braids and threads on red wool gaberdine *Gloria Cook*

Geometric shapes A geometric basis is an excellent way in which to start a design, particularly for repetition in which some formal means of spacing is necessary. All natural forms may be reduced to geometric solids, from which they are then elaborated again into pattern or flat shapes with two dimensions only. Cutting tissue paper shapes and overlapping them will give other shapes such as two shapes overlapping to give a third; folding paper and cutting or tearing will give interesting silhouettes or lace-like results according to the method employed. Spacing out

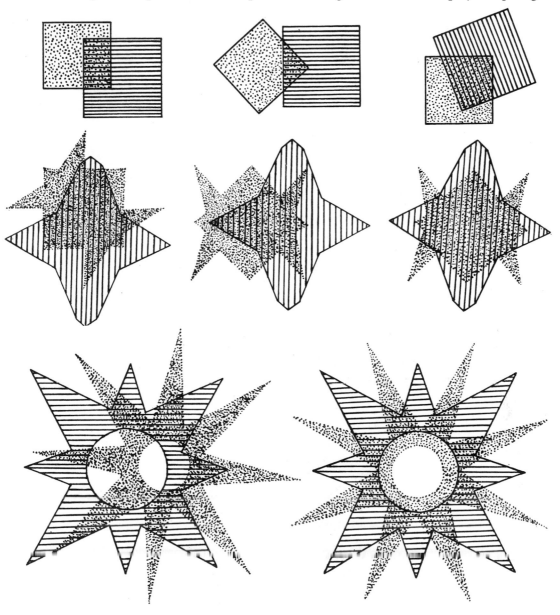

27 *Two overlapping tissue paper shapes which give a third shape and changes in colour*

actual objects on the floor or on a table within a geometric framework of string or some kind of thread, chalk lines or a grid-like arrangement will help in planning ideas on a large scale. Match sticks, drinking straws, string, buttons and coins are all useful in working out smaller patterns and linear decorations.

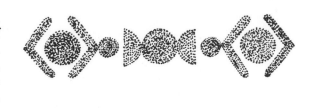

Similar geometric shapes in various sizes, cut in paper, have endless permutations. Similar ones of equal sizes may be used together to make borders and complete units of pattern, or dissimilar ones of different sizes may be moved around until pleasing arrangements occur; that is when both background and pattern shapes balance well and there is no overcrowding or awkward spaces.

The methods of execution depend on the purposes of the designs, sometimes one design might be suitable for different uses, worked in the appropriate techniques; such as outline, appliqué, pulled work, cut work, surface stitchery or canvas embroidery. The arrangements of the shapes as patterns may lead to other ideas, in developing them as buildings, or abstract design which is non-representational but not necessarily geometric or repetitive.

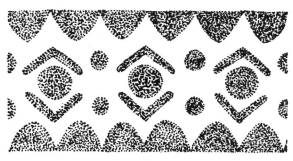

28 Cut paper shapes, showing different arrangements of similar tones and areas, negative and positive effects

29 Folded paper shapes cut to give silhouettes and lace-like patterns, suitable for basic planning of cut work and shadow work

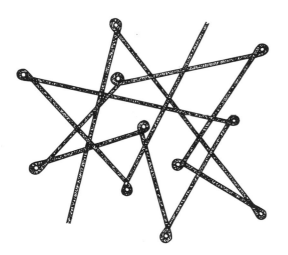

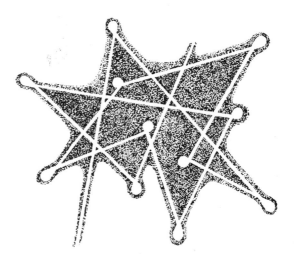

Pins or nails may be fixed in various positions on to a board and by passing threads across them, many pattern arrangements are possible, the shapes made between the threads often being of more interest than the lines but both giving ideas for embroidery.

30 Pins with threads stretched across them to make patterns showing negative and positive effects
(a) showing positions of threads
(b) the spaces made between the threads
In this way line patterns and areas of solidity may be planned

31 'Pile up'. A panel in which the use of nails with threads stretched tightly across them, gives a dynamic effect, with strength and tension directed to a particular point of interest
Anne Butler

Reference For private reference it is useful to keep a scrap book which includes reproductions, pieces of fabric and threads, pressed leaves and flowers and anything of interest for design, also a 'collectors cupboard' in which found objects and interesting natural forms may be stored, as again, it is better to work from reality whenever possible, and to supplement the scrap book information with a collection of natural objects such as shells, feathers, dried seaweeds, seed pods and seed heads, flower heads, driftwood and bark, stones, pebbles and anything of personal interest which will stimulate ideas on colour, texture and pattern.

32 Drawings from natural forms—shells, scales and skins. Concentrated study of pattern on forms such as these helps to increase ideas on both texture and colour, all of which are ideal for embroidery

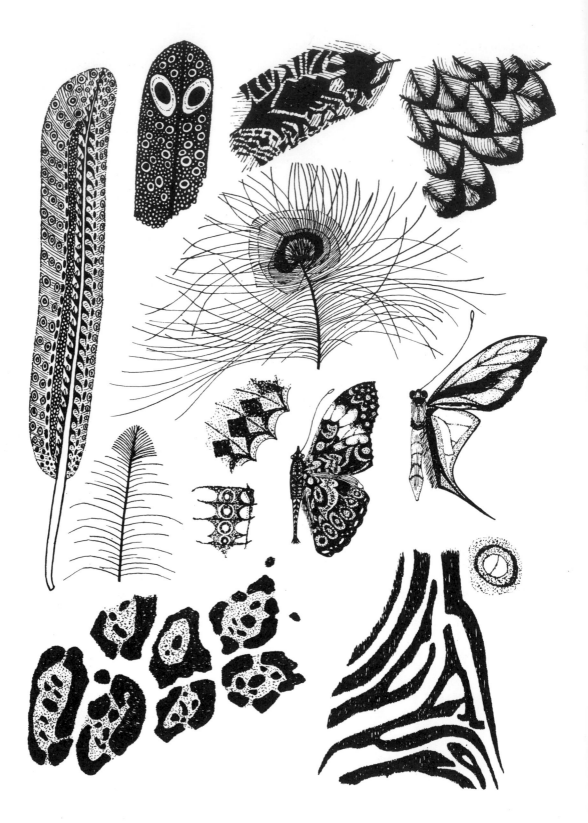

Museum study Museum study is of particular value in that ideas may be obtained by looking at other crafts. From their shapes, colours and applied decoration adaptations may be made for embroidery design. Although slavish copying is neither advisable nor suitable, many things to be found in museums have particular application to stitchery. The study of wrought iron and its continuous scrolls is a good beginning for making patterns for machine embroidery, as is some jewellery and intricate gold and silver filigree and engraving on metal. Ivory carving has textures easily translated into stitchery while archaic and mediaeval sculpture illustrates a superb conventional use of animals and figures adapted to situations and purposes and often contained in geometric shapes such as spandrels and circles. The applied patterns seen in native crafts from Africa, Polynesia, South America and other primitive and peasant populations are a source of endless ideas, many of these being built up from geometric structures and most of them based on natural forms. They are all exciting, full of vitality and examples of them are to be found in most museums. Historic embroidery is of particular interest not so much for its original pattern but from the point of view of technical skill and use of stitchery in an interesting context. It makes an absorbing study and gives a complete picture of its wide application and importance as a creative medium. Embroideries from other countries particularly of the 'peasant type' are vigorous, very lively in ideas and their use of colour and stitchery exciting as a basis for study. They are often much bolder than English embroideries both in colour and pattern and their textures are more variable but their ideas are less sophisticated which gives them a certain charm and sometimes complete naïvety.

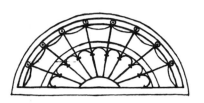

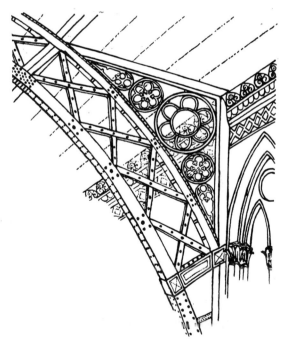

33 Drawings from naturally formed pattern. Fur, feathers and butterflies' wings, translatable into embroidery almost without alteration

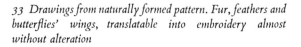

34 Wrought iron shows a continuity of line and a flowing quality, suitable for machine embroidery or quilting
    a fanlight
    an iron strip
    ironwork gate—Hampton Court
    ironwork from St Pancras Station

31

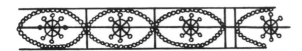

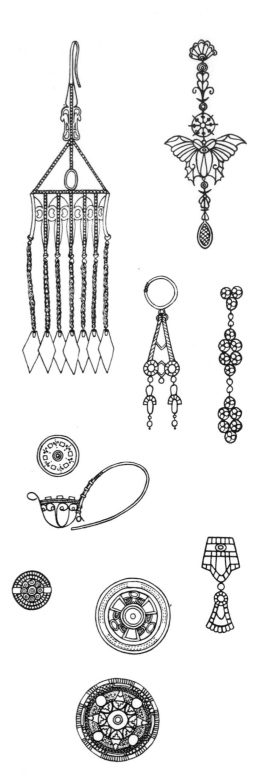

35 Patterns based on ironwork
braid or cord work
bead work and cut work
border patterns, building up from simple units as outlines
and solid shapes, some complete designs, some repetitive

36 (a) Ear-rings and brooches from India and Italy now in
the British Museum

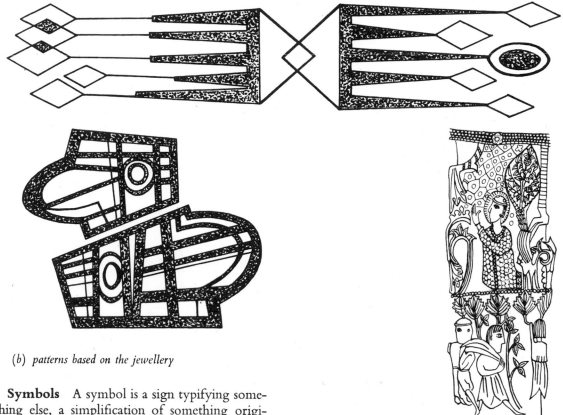

(b) *patterns based on the jewellery*

37 *Martyrdom of St Stephen and allegorical carvings in walnut. South Italian, last quarter twelfth century. The fitting of the figures in to the given shape is ingenious*
Victoria and Albert Museum

Symbols A symbol is a sign typifying something else, a simplification of something originally more complicated or abstract, such as a ring for eternity or a cross for Christianity. It was invented by primitive man to represent something or somebody, and developed into pictographs as a kind of sign writing. The symbol has many uses in design and often epitomizes an idea in simple terms. In exploring museums of applied art such as the Victoria and Albert, the York Museum and National Folk Museum of Wales the same subjects are seen occurring again and again, in examples of craft of the archaic and primitive periods to those of today. Many of the obvious natural phenomena have been used as symbols from pre-Christian times, such as the sun, moon and stars, the elements of earth, air, fire and water. Birds and fishes occur in religious and secular patterns as do the geometric shapes of circles, triangles and crosses; all of which have symbolic significance. They still retain their fascination as a basis of design, in fact these well-worn subjects possess innumerable interesting qualities from which original interpretations are possible. The human figure recurs in a variety of guises from the purely geometric to the naturalistic, in early textile design and embroidery designed by William Morris, to the abstract shapes seen in twentieth-century French tapestries and much present-day sculpture.

Although the diversity in stylization of natural form during the past is a vast field of study and cannot be gone into with any detail, it is useful to make notes of any ideas and conventions which are attractive and adaptable to embroidery today.

38 Primitive symbols taken from various sources

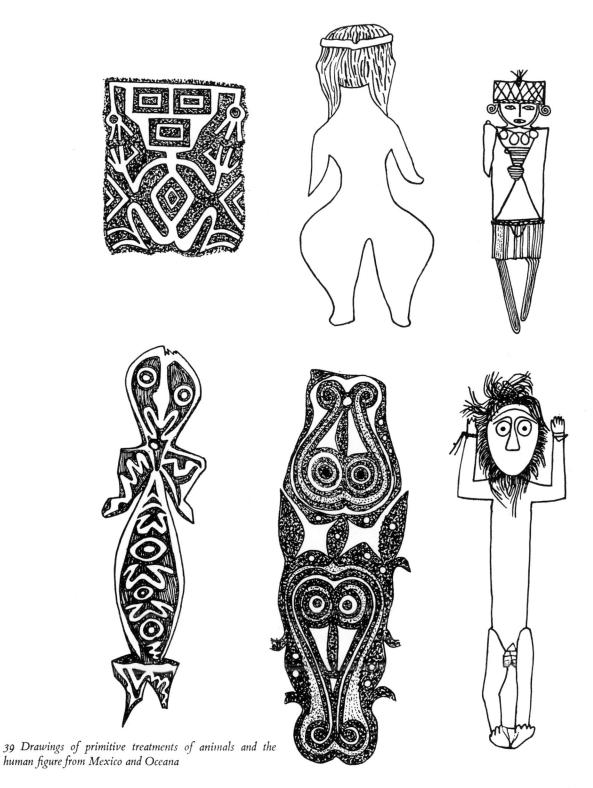

39 *Drawings of primitive treatments of animals and the human figure from Mexico and Oceana*

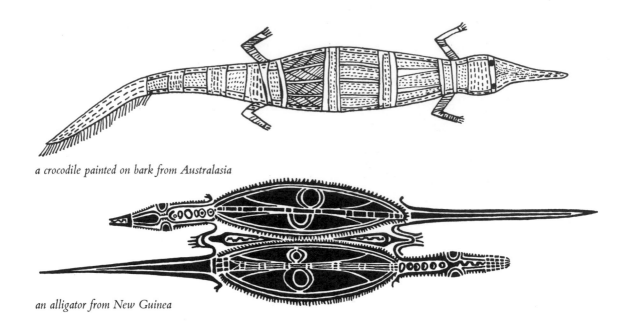

a crocodile painted on bark from Australasia

an alligator from New Guinea

40 Thebes, Tomb of Nebaman, British Museum. A conventional and repetitive treatment of animals' heads, in which an interesting pattern is made by the horns

Analysis of pattern It is valuable to be able to analyse decorative art, to define why some shapes and patterns are more pleasing than others, why some subject stylized in a Coptic woven fabric has a more pleasing character than a similar one used on a printed textile of this century, why floral embroidery of the late sixteenth century is different from that seen in eighteenth-century embroidery. By this comparison and contrast of styles and this critical outlook, appreciation in standards of design is increased. It will help in the valuation of personal efforts and should lead to a greater awareness in sensibility and selection of motifs and in the choosing of work from the past as a basis for ideas.

41 A drawing of a beetle
  an idea worked in canvas stitches
  an interpretation in beads and sequins of various kinds
  Freda Tillett

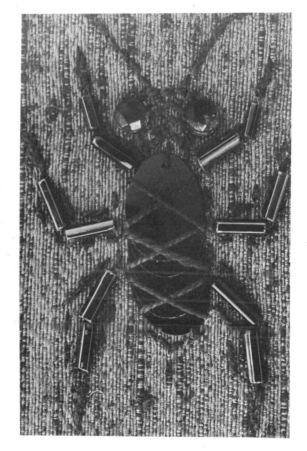

Sketch books Sketch books are the best means of recording first-hand information for future reference. They may be quite small but carried around always so that anything of interest is noted on the spot, even descriptions of colour and texture are useful when written down. With little or no previous drawing this is one of the best ways in which to start—the sketches may be peculiar at first, but this does not matter, the main thing is to look, to start to put things down on paper and to persist and to add written notes on particular points of interest. Making patterns in cut paper is an excellent beginning to design but has limitations. By learning to draw it is possible to obtain 'finesse' of shape and proportion and much more refinement of detail which is necessary in advanced work. Drawing is also an aid to 'seeing'; it will be easier to spot a better line or shape as against a poor one, a strong pattern as compared with a weak one and with practice facility improves considerably and it becomes less difficult to put down what is wanted, more accurately and with a deeper searching for structure. Imitative copying is not required but an ability to be able to show on paper essential qualities of things seen, such as directions of growth and basic underlying structure, indications of texture and pattern on natural forms and other objects, construction of solid shapes by looking at them from different angles; these facilities are invaluable and help to build up both knowledge and confidence, but remember that patience is the greatest asset as it is so easy to become discouraged when things 'don't look right'. It is a great advantage to be able to express ideas on paper and by trying out various mediums such as crayon, brush and colour, pen and ink, chalk and wax and colour, the interest in their uses, the many effects now possible with them should overcome some of the difficulties in trying to draw. Lead pencil which is a difficult medium should be avoided in the beginning as it is unsympathetic in quality, coloured ones are better, although coarser in results, and pen and ink has a fascination for some people and is useful for very fine drawing.

Natural form, environment Natural form is the most prolific source of inspiration and endless study will not exhaust its vast field, its diversity of growth, from the blade of grass to the human figure. To limit this huge and bewildering wealth of ideas, to start from a point which will enlarge observation, and help in attempts at design, gradually leading from the simple to the more complicated, a plan must be thought out so that energy is not wasted in darting from one idea to the next without orderly progress. The study of local environment is a suitable point of departure and here the observation suggested at the beginning of the chapter is extended to more detail and to searching for particular groups of shapes or growths which are not as obvious to the eye as those mentioned; whether this is in the town, country or seaside or within a combination of these backgrounds, a serious research will reveal many sources of interest adaptable to embroidery. To country dwellers natural forms are common and are often passed by. Plant, bird and animal life is observable at any time but variation in growth is affected by the seasons, luscious greenery becoming leafless stalks and dried-up seed heads, and more noticeable by its absence in the winter when trees are black and bare and the ground looks naked. Some birds and most insects also disappear and colours change considerably with the season. These are less obvious to the town dweller who has perhaps to search more rigorously at this time of the year for interesting natural details. A sketch book kept to note down seasonal changes and things seen on visiting an environment different from the usual background, comparisons of local colour and textures, particular species of plants and any points seen in these localities which are of interest, becomes invaluable as stored information for those times when working from reality is impossible.

It is wise to have an aim in mind when looking for ideas for the decoration of a specific article; perhaps for a decorative panel to hang in a certain position in a particular setting, perhaps to fill a given shape or to suit a given material. However the problem is tackled, with an aim in view, it is

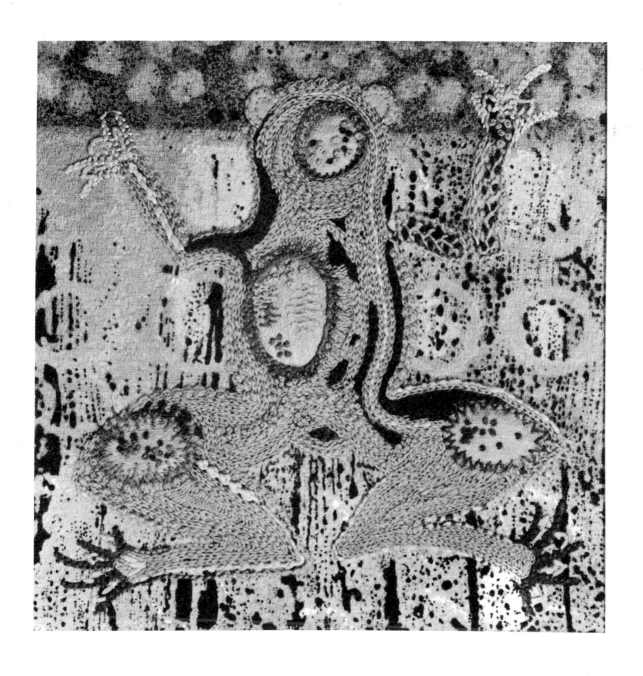

42 *A frog worked mainly in chain stitch. The idea evolved from the printed fabric, which looked 'watery'. The frog almost disappears into the background this being intentional*
Freda Tillett

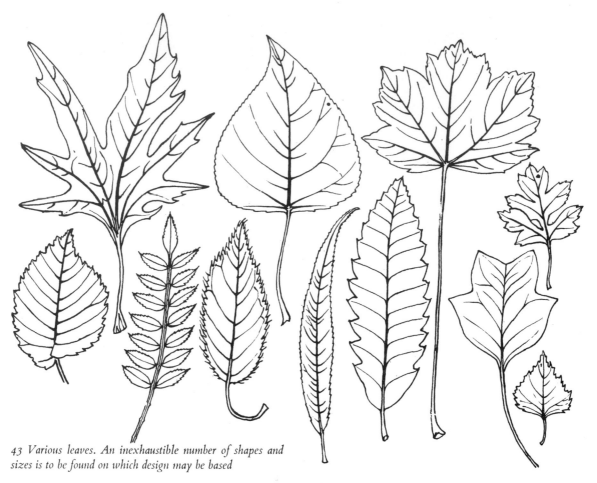

43 Various leaves. An inexhaustible number of shapes and sizes is to be found on which design may be based

easier to begin to look and to think objectively. A study of leaves is possible in any environment, gardens and allotments, woods, fields, ditches and hedges, even beaches have some plant life. Spring or summer is a suitable time for this study and a concentrated attempt to draw the variety of leaves found on an allotment or those in the hedgerow and ditch in a country lane will yield many more shapes than would have been thought possible. At the same time things other than leaves will be noticed, netting over strawberries, bean sticks, the shapes of different bushes, the difference in texture of bark on tree trunks, the delicacy of some weeds, the sharp prickles and twisted branches of some hedgerows, the dark rich green of plants growing in a damp ditch. All these observations add up to an accumulation of more knowledge, a detailed and closer perception and

more resources from which to develop ideas for design.

Each season has special interests, during the spring and summer, trees, leaves and flowers make worthwhile study, towards the autumn the seeds and berries, fruits and vegetables give other ideas. Dried seeds and flowers should be collected for inspiration, used in the winter months when it is too cold to work out of doors.

The growth and diversity of shape and character of trees are more clearly seen when they are leafless and they provide a basis for all kinds of design, particularly of abstract shapes and here again, a well-filled sketch book is necessary as these should contain sufficient drawings to give ideas until the next summer.

Rocks, cliffs and stones, their strata, weathering and colour are more difficult to indicate on paper

44 Plants, mainly weeds, which are the basis of many ideas for design

but are a valuable source for study, suggesting ideas for embroidery from large wall hangings in appliqué to fine machine embroidered cushions with decorations based on sand and pebbles. Their layerings and textures show sufficient natural pattern to be extracted for many purposes, they are often almost abstract designs without alteration of shapes or redistribution in planning and are quite beautiful in colour and sufficient to give inspiration for many subtle schemes.

Microscope From the large to the small, the variety of shape is infinite and if a microscope is available small particles of rock seen under the lens show marvellous colours and shapes, invisible to the naked eye. Cellular structures and sections of plants are a source of inspiration viewed in this way. If a microscope is unobtainable there are a number of books published with superb enlarged photographs taken from these microscopic sections, both in black and white and colour.

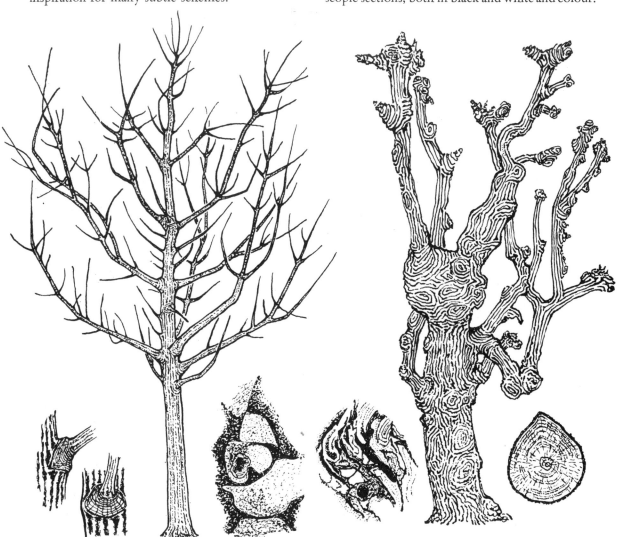

45 *Tree forms. Without leaves the general structure of growth is seen more easily. Details of cross sections and bark give ideas for texture and patterns*

46 The shape of a tree with its silhouette and pattern seen between the branches

to give clear shadows, should be fairly close to a background of paper as their silhouettes will then appear darker and their positions can be painted in with a brush and ink or water colour. Strong sunlight on glass objects throws beautiful shadows and glasses may be superimposed one in front of the other to give intricate, lace-like effects and patterns, which are sometimes so decorative that they may be translated into embroidery without alteration, sometimes shadows of different objects may be painted on top of one another, forming other shapes by their overlapping. With experiment exciting grids and network patterns can be made with wire and string or cane, overlaid one on another to make even more complicated patterns. By moving the grids around to alter the shadows and the sizes of the holes produced by the overlapping of wire over cane infinite variations are possible.

It should be possible to obtain some of them from the local libraries when direct observation is impractical and is a legitimate means of obtaining ideas. Books showing botanical sections might be used to supplement these photographs even when drawing from reality.

Magnifying glass A magnifying glass is invaluable as an aid to any designer. By its use parts of plants may be seen enlarged, textures become more visible and insignificant detail appears quite exciting, small patterns may be enlarged and seen more easily for representing on paper. This general use of magnification of things normally difficult to see, opens up another field of vision and helps in looking even more carefully at details.

Shadows As another means of simplification of form and an appreciation of flat shape, shadows are valuable in design. Objects are moved at various distances away from a strong lamp and according to this distance their shadows can be altered, being shortened or elongated. The objects,

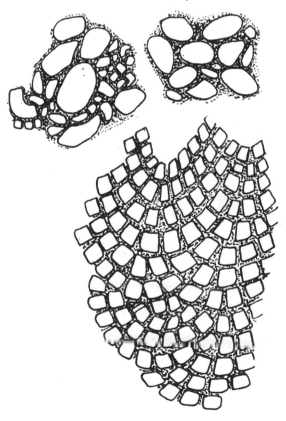

47 Stones from paths, from the beach and granite sett cobbles

43

48 *Stone walls—part of an appliqué panel based on dry-stone walling* *Marjorie Preece*

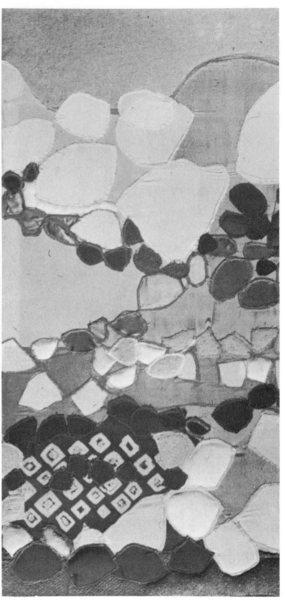

49 *Ideas from walls and stones* *Goldsmiths*

50 *Stones and pebbles — an appliqué panel in machine embroidery with some padding to give depth* *Goldsmiths*

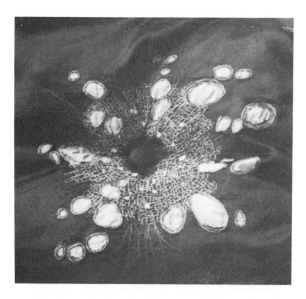

51 Machine embroidered cushion cover. Stones and sand
Angela Brandreth-Cook

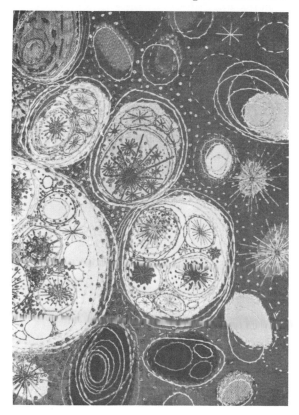

52 Part of a panel, the idea derived from cellular structures
Pauline Watson

Animals and birds Anything which moves swiftly requires greater concentration to understand. Constant observation under different circumstances is necessary in order to become acquainted with the basic structure underlying action. Animals and birds, both wild and tame possess interesting shapes, patterns and textures, their main characteristics are litheness and sinuosity with their heads and bodies merging smoothly and their vigour of movement depending on the placing of the legs and paws in relation to the bodies and the sizes and positions of their heads. Animals and birds are easily adapted to fit geometric shapes, as their suppleness may be curved and twisted into all manner of positions, and if their basic silhouettes are reduced to geometric ones this will help in simplifying their proportions; patterns and textures are more easily studied from stuffed examples if available, but it is by constant observation that their movements and individual characteristics are understood so that these may be used successfully in design. It might be noted here that patterns on birds and animals, although often for camouflage also help to intensify the rhythm of movement and structure by their placing and distribution on the forms. This is useful in design if strong movement is required. Colour is often part of camouflage, when the animals and birds merge into their natural surroundings but it may also be strong and brilliant as in the case of male birds such as the peacock, when it is a means of attraction to the female. Details of pattern and texture on animals and birds are interesting for interpreting into embroidered surfaces, particularly if enlarged and developed into complete units of design as then they will suggest many ways of working with ingenuity in the choice of stitches and threads.

Reptiles, fishes and insects Reptiles, fishes and insects have similar properties, interesting shapes and surface qualities, in fact some of their textures could be translated into embroidery without alteration, their patterns are so perfect that they do not require rearranging, but the scale could be altered, both pattern and texture being enlarged or reduced to give effects different from reality.

45

Human figure The human figure is the most complicated yet one of the most interesting of subjects for adaptation to design, it may be reduced to simple terms and to an almost geometric pattern, it may be contorted into many positions, elongated, shortened, widened, details may be enlarged or decreased according to the character required, such as a very small head on a large body, great length of limbs as compared with reality, to give elegance, or breadth of torso to create an appearance of strength. It has been a favourite theme for decoration in many countries and from pre-Christian times, the human head being of particular fascination as its features are easily adapted to flat pattern and by varying their proportions and distribution, completely different effects are created.

The same rules apply to the study of the human figure as to the observation of birds and animals. It should be seen in violent action, in repose, in normal everyday positions and examined from all angles, sketches being made whenever possible from life. If the articulation of the figure is to be understood, it is helpful to make drawings from the skeleton as this will give some understanding of both movement and silhouette. In simplifying the figure for design, unwanted details are discarded and those which indicate character and movement can be made of greater importance or exaggerated in scale or shape. This entails a great deal of observation as only with thorough knowledge is this elimination possible as is the emphasis of the right parts to create vitality and individuality according to the idea in mind.

Man-made forms From small tools to large buildings, ideas for design using man-made forms as a basis are so many that the most important consideration is what to avoid. This may depend on the purpose of the embroidery as quite obviously some subjects are more suitable for certain purposes than others; small articles such as safety pins, screws, scissors, cotton reels and kitchen tools have pleasant shapes, watch and clock interiors, machinery of all kinds, wheels of various sizes and mechanical transport never lose their interest. Parts of the larger and more intricate apparatus possess sufficient wealth of detail from which exciting decoration may be planned, the small cog wheels in watches and clocks and the chain wheels and pedals of bicycles could be planned to make complete designs or could be built up into repetitive border patterns worked in thick, chunky stitchery by hand with fine lines of machining to complement this. Shapes may be cut directly in paper from the actual objects, but if a permanent record of them is required and if their structures are to be remembered and understood it is better to make direct sketches for future reference.

Things seen against the skyline in silhouette, chimneys and roof tops, cranes, scaffolding, bridges and different levels of buildings show simplified line and mass, suitable for bold embroidery. More detail is found in brick walls, cracked pavements, cobblestones, wrought iron balconies and fanlights, in fact any street is a source of information and ideas.

Once the habit of observation becomes part of everyday life ideas multiply, and with practice their translation into design for embroidery becomes easier. This section cannot give more than a few suggestions from which an inexhaustible number of ideas may be worked out. Other sources of design will naturally lead on from exploring some of those already mentioned.

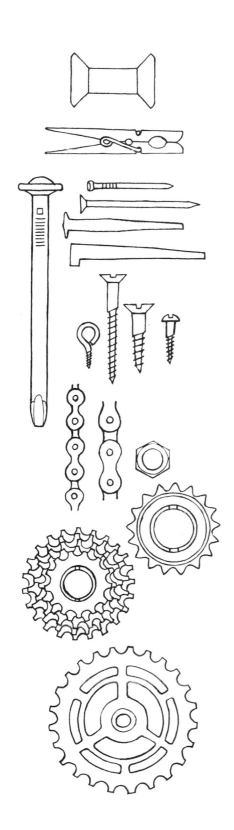

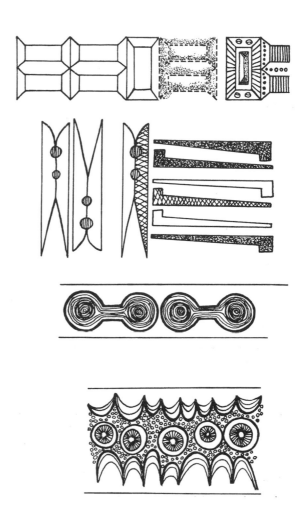

53 Man-made objects: cotton reels, pegs, nails, screws, bicycle chain parts, cog wheels
    a design based on the reels, English quilting, beads
    idea based on clothes pegs
    on nails
    on the bicycle chains
    on the bicycle chains

Design

Several apt expressions which might relate to any art or craft have a particular meaning when applied to the embroiderer. Moholy-Nagy says in *The New Vision and Abstract of an Artist* on 'the function of the artist—art is the senses' grindstone, sharpening the eyes, the mind and the feelings. Art has an educational and formative ideological function—the artist interprets ideas and concepts through his own media' and again 'the artist may mix techniques. In fact he can do whatever he pleases, providing he masters his means and has something to express.'

Application An appreciation of design and an understanding of it is the basis of all successful craftwork. It involves a knowledge of materials, processes and the proper uses of tools pertaining to the craft. There are no short cuts, as observation and the application of knowledge gained from it is the basis on which personal interpretation from reality is developed, together with individual choice of materials and use of them to create original work.

Design without application is as pointless as technique without aesthetic consciousness. In order to understand fully the range of possibilities in all styles of embroidery, constant experiment, exploration of materials and ways and means of approach to it are necessary.

In this craft neither design nor technique can be isolated. There are certain limitations which must be understood before designing for specific purposes, also limitations in what is possible by using materials and threads. The invention of new ones in various synthetic combinations with qualities different from those of natural fibres means that there must be a constant awareness of their possibilities and the differences in handling them. The ever-changing fashions in styles and fabrics demand a knowledge of current trends as embroidery is the decoration of a surface already provided and should enhance this, or there is little point in carrying it out. Although the fundamental principles of design are constant, emphasis in style changes and is accomplished by a variety of means.

Meaning The word 'design' means different things to different people but is essentially a deliberate planning as against an arbitrary or accidental one. It involves an orderly approach to a problem and a mental picture of the whole idea, within which there may be many divisions. It includes shape, colour, tone and texture and is a matter largely of contrasts and tensions which give vitality, large against small, light against dark, rough against smooth, wide against narrow. In fact all design must have contrasting qualities if it is to possess vitality. Design is not just some pattern, placed at random on a background. An enclosing shape or structure is necessary before the idea can be planned and developed; it may be a small spot on a square of fabric but the square is the enclosing shape and the position of the spot in relation to this is important, a vase may have applied decoration but the shape of the vase is determined before any pattern is put on it. The overall shape of anything and the placing of the decoration in relation to its area is a part of any design and cannot be thought of separately. In fact balance of area against space, of shape against line, of repetition versus variation are all essential points which require a great deal of thought and experiment, if the finished work is to be successful.

Approach Some people have an instinctive feeling for pattern and colour often termed 'a sense of design', others achieve it by hard work, trial and error. Patience, constant scrapping of ideas and often disappointment in the initial stages must be accepted when starting from scratch. The main point is to remember that work must progress from the simple to the complex and not to try to design beyond the first stage until that one is understood. It is possible to become a proficient designer providing that progress is maintained from the elementary approach at the beginning to the high standard of achievement attainable by a fully trained artist.

Quality and pitfalls Embroidery is essentially a two-dimensional craft and in designing for it the third dimension and true perspective may be disregarded. This does not mean that the work when finished looks flat, as both texture and colour may be used to give a richness and intensity and a depth different from that of a painting. With the great variety of textures and surface qualities which are an inherent part of embroidery, with slight padding, cutting away, and techniques that emphasize tone, this depth is easily created but that of a two-dimensional quality and not of realism. This difference in approach requires as much thought and practice as does painting and sculpture, and is a case of working from another angle with other materials. Embroidery has exciting aspects which should be exploited to the full and it is only now that this is beginning to happen and the enormous breadth of the craft

and its implications are being realized. It is easy to obtain a semblance of painting in stitchery and appliqué but it is a waste of time, as to paint is relatively quicker; try to avoid this imitation of another media and to think in terms of the many variations and effects possible in embroidery. There is a tendency to embroider freely on the machine, using the needle as a pen and 'drawing' in a rather realistic fashion, so producing neither good embroidery nor good design. Splodges of fabric are applied to backgrounds and merged into them with machine stitchery so that a lithographic effect is achieved. Overlaid nets are employed in the same way and give similar results and although these effects are interesting they are misleading as they do not emphasize the true qualities of the craft. Rigid rules cannot be decreed and it would be wrong if they were, but these effects may be modified, in fact avoided. Free machine stitchery can be beautifully designed and there are many more facets to its range of textures than might be imagined. Combined with hand embroidery the two techniques are often more interesting than when used separately and experiment in this field of design should be encouraged.

Creative thought What is creative embroidery if not a trying out of original design and methods of approach not previously attempted? The ability to choose the right materials and threads for a particular purpose, the most suitable techniques to use, the type and position of every stitch sewn into the fabric so that each has as much meaning as a mark on paper in drawings of a high standard, is surely an interpretation of this term and results in a design developed into something vitally alive and far better than the original conception, which can only be taken so far on paper.

Methods of procedure It is impossible and a waste of time to put down on paper a careful painting of a finished embroidery. This is not necessary nor are the exact representations of stitches required. The resultant piece of work, faithfully copied, would be boring to carry out and probably lack vitality when finished. In most cases it is sufficient just to indicate the main

lines and areas of the design before working it
out, but this depends on whether the embroidery
is for personal pleasure only, or whether the design
is commissioned and has to be approved and
passed by another person, in which case a more
detailed idea must be presented. The suggestions
given here for methods of approaching design
are suitable for different styles of embroidery and
scales of work and should give sufficient indication of procedure to help in planning most ideas.
Details on specific techniques and limitations in
making designs for them are given on pages 165
and 191.

It is assumed when working out the basic ideas
that they are not dissociated from the materials
and threads to be used, and the textures and colours
to be chosen, as all designs will include these
although not necessarily shown in outline
drawings. The probable method of work must be
decided upon too as otherwise some patterns
might be unsuitable for the techniques chosen
for the embroidery. Before commencing to
design, pieces of fabric should be available with
as many varieties of threads as can be collected,
as it is impossible to complete an idea satisfactorily
without having them around for reference.

Paper cutting There are several ways in
which design may be evolved, one of the most
direct being by paper cutting or tearing.

This method requires:

1 Newspaper.
2 Some plain papers contrasting in tones of
black, greys and white, such as kitchen-shelf
paper which is cheap, wrapping papers, or
tissue paper.
3 Paste, glue and/or dressmakers' pins.
4 Threads or strings and cords.
5 Tailors' chalk in dark and light colours, and
coloured pencils.

The main idea is obtained by means of cutting
or tearing paper shapes in one of the tones of
paper. These are laid on a contrasting toned paper
background and shifted around until the arrangement looks satisfactory. They may be re-cut,
enlarged in size, discarded or added to if the first
planning is not pleasing, but until they are right,

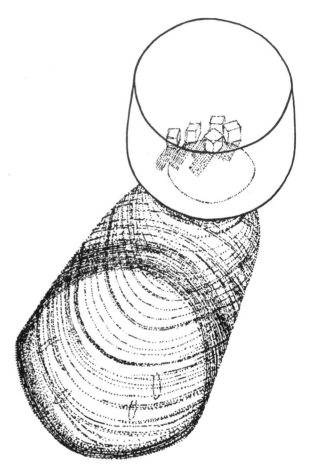

*54 A shadow cast by a glass bowl in strong sunlight, on to a
Formica table top. The shadow could be interpreted in thick
and thin lines of couching*

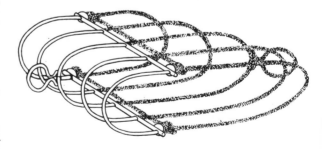

*55 A toast rack on its side—the drawing is turned round.
This shows a simple shadow pattern from a complicated
object, and might be an idea for Italian quilting or narrow
braid appliqué*

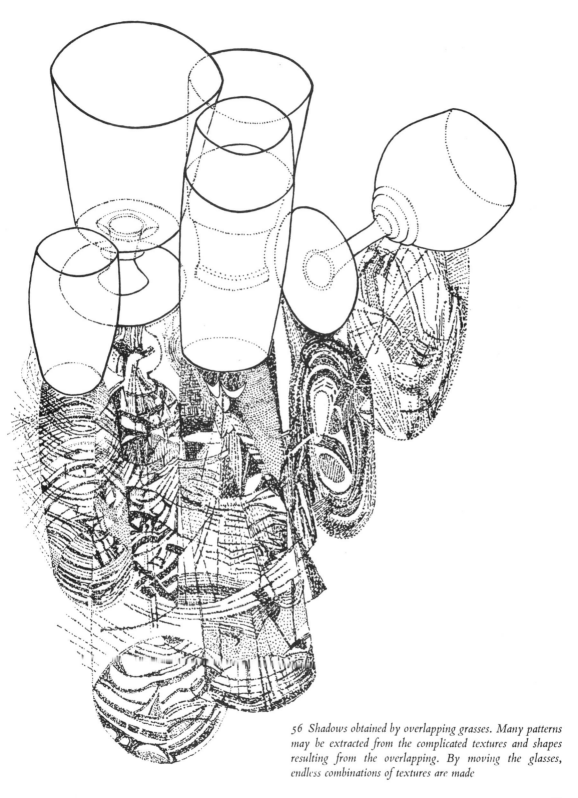

56 *Shadows obtained by overlapping grasses. Many patterns may be extracted from the complicated textures and shapes resulting from the overlapping. By moving the glasses, endless combinations of textures are made*

that is, well spaced and of good proportionate shapes do not attempt the next stage.

It might be said 'When is a design satisfactory, how is it possible to know which is a better arrangement than another, as a beginner, and when is it right?' A great deal depends on personal taste but if several sets of similar paper shapes are cut at a time, each design can be planned differently within a similar area. It should be easier in this way to select the most pleasing arrangement from these and then to re-cut unsatisfactory shapes. Try to analyse why one planning is better than the others as this all helps in learning to see and 'feel' whether a design is right. The shapes may be too similar in area, too crowded within the given space, pushed into a corner, too evenly spaced giving a monotonous equality between background and pattern, they may be too broken up, harsh and awkward making background space poor in shape, or there may be too many unrelated ones put together. Whenever patterns are weak, try to find the reasons for this. If the cut paper pattern is as well arranged as possible, lines connecting shapes, if required, may be indicated temporarily with threads or string. Shapes of another tone and smaller than those already cut may be placed within or on top of the first ones to indicate further divisions of pattern or they may be larger and placed behind the original ones to expand the pattern, the final result being pasted or pinned to the background; with coloured pencil or chalk lines drawn under the threads to mark the positions of the lines permanently. Other details may be added with more paper cutting or with crayon until the whole idea is taken as far as necessary for working out in embroidery. Finally, if the shapes are pasted down a careful tracing of the finished design is made which is transferred to the material by any appropriate method.

Another way using simple paper cutting which does not involve so much initial detail but perhaps more drawing later, is to pin down the basic shapes of the main pattern onto the paper instead of sticking them, draw round them with chalk or coloured pencil, indicate any lines as previously in thread or string, then draw under them,

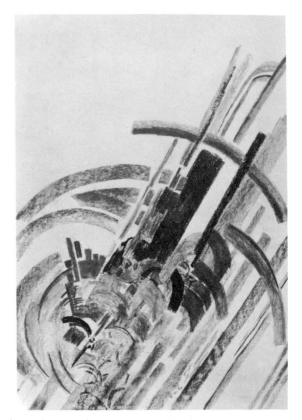

57 Bottles with shadows overlapping in sunlight. Charcoal and coloured chalks drawn directly on to the paper over the shadows, which continue to change as the sun moves
Ioné Dorrington

removing the pieces of paper and thread leaving an outline drawing on the background paper. More shapes and details may be suggested in chalk, paint or coloured pencil until the design is sufficiently indicated to be transferred to the material by tacking through the lines on the paper straight on to the fabric then tearing away the paper, or by any other suitable method if the original design is to be kept, or if it is too intricate for tacking.

Very bold designs without detail, simple outline shapes and some geometric patterns may be given a preliminary planning on a paper background, with string and cut outs. The paper shapes are then used as pattern shapes and trans-

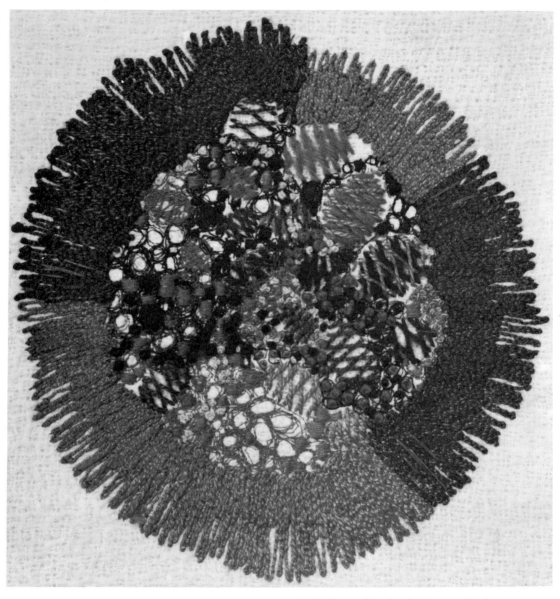

58 Machine and hand embroidery combined
Isobel Chapman

ferred to the fabric background, arranged as they were previously on the paper, pinned into position and drawn round with tailors' chalk as are the string lines. The shapes and string are removed, the chalk lines are stitched in more permanently with tacking thread, so that when the embroidery is commenced the design does not disappear, thus eliminating the intermediate stage of transferring from tracing paper to material. This method is not suitable for small patterns with intricate details where careful and finer cutting and more drawing is required. When the transferring must be done with absolute accuracy and in great detail, the pricking and pouncing method is most satisfactory and the only reliable way of ensuring exactitude.

This is done as follows:

1 Trace the design on to tracing paper.
2 Place it, right side up, on a thick blanket or pad of felt.
3 Prick holes with a needle about $\frac{1}{10}$ to $\frac{1}{8}$ inch apart all round the outline.
4 Sandpaper away the rough paper caused by the pricks.
5 Pin the fabric, taut and flat, on to a board.
6 Place the tracing paper over it and with a soft pad rub in the pounce (proportionate mixture of powdered charcoal and cuttlefish).
7 Remove the tracing.
8 Blow off the surplus powder.
9 Paint over the outline of dots with fine lines in dark or light water-colour paint.

For very elaborate designs, many tracings may have to be made from the basic paper cutting, before the drawings are complete. Each one may have slight alterations, shifting of shapes, turning these round, with modifications of size, until the result is satisfactory from every viewpoint.

Geometric shapes such as circles, squares and triangles may be cut in paper, arranged and pinned directly on to fabric, marked round the edges with chalk lines which are then tacked over for permanency, or painted in with watercolour on smooth fine surfaces. Folding of paper shapes and then cutting patterns into these will give more intricate and lace-like results, both the negative and positive shapes being used for different purposes. By overlapping two tissue paper shapes a third shape is made. This method is full of possibilities as by slight movement one way or another the third shape may be changed, more shapes may be overlapped over the first two until elaborate patterns are built up which may be worked in outlines or solidly or in a combination of both outlines and solid areas.

Colour and paste A more advanced method in planning a design is a combination of paper cutting or tearing and colour. The main shapes are again cut in paper and moved around until a satisfactory arrangement is made. They may be cut in coloured paper, tissue or opaque, or

in newspaper which is painted afterwards. The main idea in using paper is to produce good, well arranged shapes which are stuck down to the paper background after moving them around and trying them in various positions rather than drawing with a pencil on paper and wasting time rubbing out until they are satisfactory. The design is developed from this arrangement with brush and ink or some other form of colour in which details are added to complete it as far as necessary before working. Chalks or pencils can be used but they have not always the strength of paint. Texture may be indicated and a suggestion of stitchery if the finished design is to be shown to a client. Paste can be mixed with water-colour paint, allowed to become tacky on the paper then scraped off in parts to suggest roughness, or broken colour. With a fine point or a blunt one (a match stick), paste can be scraped off in lines to indicate linear stitchery of various thicknesses from machine embroidery to coarse hand embroidery. Rice or seeds such as bird seed and sunflower seeds glued down will indicate knotted and knobbly stitchery, string or thread may be glued down to suggest linear patterns, in fact any methods are legitimate in indicating design on paper as long as the required effect is achieved.

It must be repeated that in any design the spacing of both lines and shapes in relation to one another is all important, also that those shapes between pattern and lines are as significant as the shapes themselves, if there is overcrowding or too much emptiness in the wrong places awkward and poor decoration results.

Basic planning By now it will be realized that a sound idea is necessary before any design is commenced, but that also there are points which must be known before it is possible to go any further; these are:

1 The purpose for which the design is intended.
2 The choice of materials and threads suitable for the purpose.
3 The choice of technique or techniques most suitable for carrying out the design.

Take point 1 for example; the design may be

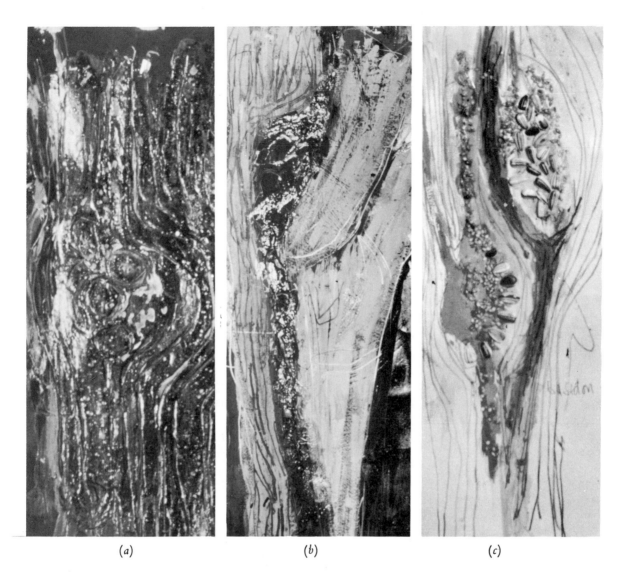

| (a) | (b) | (c) |

required for the decoration of household linen, presumably the article must launder, it must be strong, therefore the embroidery must become a part of the fabric, so eliminating certain techniques such as appliqué and loose stitchery. The article may be a tablecloth on which the placing of the pattern and its colour are important as the cloth is used in conjunction with china, cutlery and food, all of which have colour, often pattern. According to the placing of the embroidery on the cloth it will be seen easily or may be almost obscured. If it is not to be seen, why embroider the cloth at all? A wall hanging may be required to go in a

59 Three ways in which ideas representing designs from bark have been interpreted on paper

(a) *paste and colour with fine lines scratched into the paint by a needle. This method gives the effect of machine embroidery*

(b) *paste and paint and cut paper to give a thick effect, suitable for hand embroidery*

(c) *various sized birdseeds used to represent french knots and cable chain stitch on a painted ground with pencil lines to represent machine stitching* Brenda Holmes

definite setting. Here colour and texture are of the utmost importance as by the choice of these, the result will sink or give significance to the room,

*60 A design shown to scale with a portion drawn full size for
a prospective client　　　　　　　　　　　　Mary Hilder
The working out of the design is shown in figure 279*

but technique may be free as the hanging will not receive hard wear and can be cleaned. On the other hand the design must be as good as possible as on a wall it will be seen by many people, all its faults will glare out and its scale will probably be such that it cannot be ignored.

If all these considerations are taken into account before a design is started, a great deal of time is saved as certain ideas, materials and methods are immediately found to be unsuitable for the purpose in mind.

The type of pattern for the article in question is the next point to decide. This may to some extent depend upon the size of the work. A large wall hanging would be unsuitable covered with small repetitive patterns; an embroidered cushion cover on the other hand could be charming with the small units placed in the right order on it such as an all-over pattern or a surrounding border of shapes which might be basically repetitive with variations of stitchery, or shapes similar in scale but non-repetitive in detail.

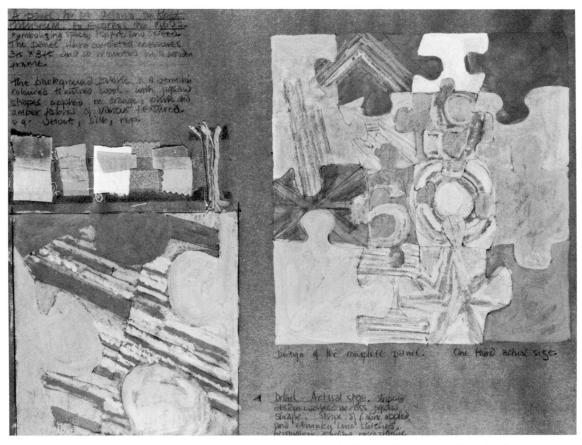

61 *A sketch design for a panel. The embroidery is shown in*
figure 300 Isobel Hare

Scale These points raise the question of scale as the size of the embroidery is interrelated with the technique. Very fine stitchery with one strand of silk is quite out of place for the working of a large wall hanging, which is to be seen at a distance and must be bold and basically simple. It may contain one or two small spots of brilliant, fine silk stitchery in contrast to the rest of the work but these would serve to enhance the coarseness of scale of other threads used. On the other hand, a christening robe designed with 6 inch circular floral motifs would probably swamp the child wearing it, even if embroidered finely; the pattern should be small and delicate as a young baby is not very big.

In designing for large pieces of work it is practical to make a careful drawing to scale, then to have it enlarged by the photostat method up to perhaps twelve times the original size. The complete copy may come back in separate parts, but this 'blowing up' eliminates squaring up and a great deal of wasted time.

If a scale design is to be shown to a client it is a good idea to present with this a small portion drawn to full size in which the proposed method of work and suggested stitchery are indicated in their final form. A mistake often made is to draw a small sketch design for embroidery and to indicate the stitchery on it as for a full-scale design, in other words, working size. This gives quite a false idea for a final design of a much larger scale and the suggestions for working out details would be inappropriate as they stand.

62 Drawings of objects to show the translation from three-dimensional reality to two-dimensional pattern
  a chair and simplified shapes
  a bed and ideas evolved from its basic shape

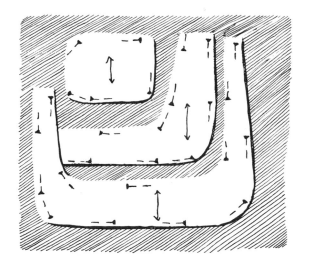
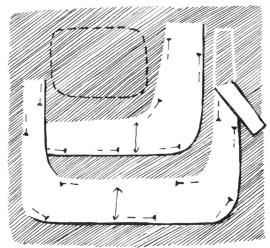

63 *Shapes pinned down, drawn round with chalk, then removed from the background. The outlines of these shapes are then tacked*

Geometric structure A logical way to start designing for embroidery is from the geometric structure of fabric by working from the cloth onwards, trying out different types of fabric and choosing various ways of building up stitch patterns on the counted threads on woven or woven and printed backgrounds. A great deal can be learnt about threads, textures and materials in this way as well as the methods by which patterns grow step by step and become intricate. Small experimental pieces of work are most helpful at this stage in order to try out effects, the variety obtainable with combinations of fabrics, different threads and stitches being infinite.

Patterned fabrics

Checks Checked ginghams or other cloths woven in squares, plaids or stripes have regular repetitive patterns, some being large enough to contain complete motifs of embroidery. The appearance of the cloth itself may be altered by cutting pieces on the cross and applying these to the straight grain or by pleating and folding. Checks of different sizes may be used together, such as a $\frac{1}{2}$ inch check gingham with an $\frac{1}{8}$ inch check, or stripes combined with checks. With this experiment it is better to limit the fabrics to similarity of colour, such as a black and white striped one with a black and white check. Confusion results if colour, manipulation of fabric and stitchery are all tried at once on one piece of work. Stitchery in one of the colours of the cloth in a thick thread such as 'anchor soft' or perle give the best results as the aim is to intensify one of these colours and to change the tonal character of the cloth in part, to one darker or lighter than the original. By blocking out the black squares with white thread, on a black and white gingham perhaps some of the grey ones too, an area of white texture results. This must be done with solid stitchery and thick threads, the thin stranded cotton cross-stitch patterns often seen are of no use as they do little to cover the fabric. Plaids are a good basis for repetitive motifs, if spaced widely spots or squares of stitchery can be worked in the spaces between the lines. Coins, beads, buttons and paper shapes help here in planning the sizes of repetitive motifs which can be developed into rich stitch patterns within the plaids. Some of the lines of the plaids may have strengthening stitchery to emphasize or to broaden them into stripes.

64 A child's dress in black and white gingham, with a folded border cut on the cross. A beginning in using materials in an interesting way
Susan White
Rachel McMillan College of Education

66 Gingham blouse with the white squares blocked out by stitchery in black anchor soft cotton. Knotted cable chain spanish feather stitch and cross stitch used to give a wide braid effect
Penelope Collins

65 A border with $\frac{1}{2}$ inch checks cut on the cross, applied to an $\frac{1}{8}$ inch checked gingham, and embroidered in black and white perle

67 Gingham cuff of a blouse, with an embroidered band applied on the cross of the fabric

68 *A checked border on a plain fabric embroidered to give a braid effect. Threaded wheels and linked chain worked in perle and anchor soft cotton*

69 *Machine and hand embroidery combined, to emphasize a border of gingham which could be applied to a plain- or self-coloured fabric. Cable stitch in anchor soft cotton and fine machine cotton combined*

70 *Gingham pleated and secured with stitchery in anchor soft cotton and perle. One side of the pleating conceals the black, one side the white checks*

71 (a) *Checks embroidered in knotted cable chain stitch.*

(b) *Stripes arranged to form chevrons suitable for dress or household articles. French knots, knotted cable chain and twisted-chain*

Stripes Striped fabrics have qualities similar to those of checks and plaids with greater variation in widths of patterns which may be cut and arranged in several ways, some very wide ones being suitable as backgrounds for the planning of complete patterns. They may be pleated to show more of one colour than another, cut with the pieces re-assembled as chevrons, used in bands horizontally on the vertical striped backgrounds and as straight line guides they are an excellent means of building up patterns entirely in stitchery, where the design is made by the choice of open with closed stitches, narrow stitches with wide stitches, knotted stitches with flat, smooth stitches. The selection of the most suitable threads is important, coarse and fine ones used together giving variation and interest to the results. The choice of stitchery and threads is the basis on which attractive decoration is evolved in this way.

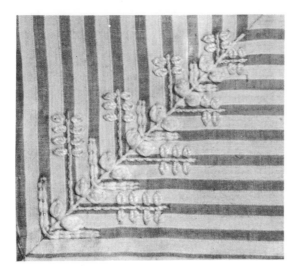

72 An embroidered corner on a yoke of striped fabric

73 Horizontal stripes on a vertical background stripe. The stitchery is simple but has sufficient emphasis to give the result individuality

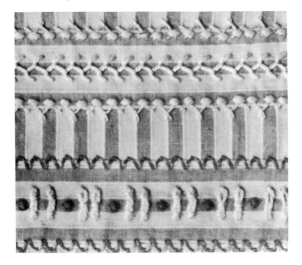

74 Horizontal stripes in pink and white on a vertical striped background, embroidered in white and pink threads

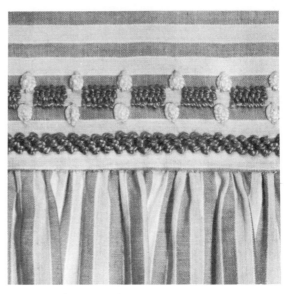

75 Striped fabric used for dress—a gathered yoke, skirt or cuff, with embroidery to emphasize the seam line. Raised chain band, single knotted cable chain and cretan stitch

Stitch patterns It is possible to use one stitch and by altering its width and the thickness of thread with which it is worked, to obtain a complete and varied border pattern. Herringbone with its wide diversity of composite stitches is a good example of this, buttonhole another. Good striped and border patterns, without any drawing, but careful selection of stitchery and threads can be worked on a firm medium-weight background fabric, using surface embroidery. Thick cotton threads with fine ones in self colour worked on muslin or organdie give rich effects similar to those found on early nineteenth-century Indian muslin dresses, although in this use of pure stitchery no floral design is involved. On a fabric with easily counted threads borders of pulled or drawn stitches alternating with solid satin stitch or other surface stitching are effective. Raised chain band or portuguese border worked in conjunction with straight thin lines of couching, stem or chain or in machine stitching in self colour or in one colour contrasting with the background, are sufficient without preliminary drawing, for simple decorations on dress, as braid-like results are obtained with them, as long as the raised stitches are worked in thick threads. Uninteresting stitch patterns are often the result of using too thin threads and poor combinations of stitchery, together with several colours, whereas one colour might have been better and given a more concentrated appearance. Dorset feather stitch when worked in many colours is ruined, as its charm is in its texture which is lost with the multiplicity of colours seen in its use today.

Spots Spots are usually printed, regularly or irregularly, of similar or different colours and in many sizes, from pinpricks to those 6 inches in diameter or more. Do not choose fabrics with those too closely printed as it is then difficult to embroider round the edges of the spots, which may be left plain but linked with embroidery, they may be enlarged or reduced in size, by working outside their edges or inside with stitchery in the colour of the spot or in that of the background. Spots may be made by drawing round coins, cotton reels, cups and saucers or even dinner plates, according to the scale required. Some of the very large ones seen printed on fabric, which would be termed circles, are ideal for building up complete stitch patterns for the decoration of curtains and hangings or as a basis for elaborate design. Large spots may be applied to backgrounds in contrasting fabrics if required (see also *The circle*, page 79).

Plain fabrics, counting threads   Plain fabrics with well-defined warp and weft are excellent for building up patterns entirely in stitchery by counting threads in some sort of order. Great variety is obtainable by a wide range of repetition rather than a narrow one and no drawn fabric or drawn thread embroidery need be a monotonous working of the same stitches over large areas. According to the method used and the effect desired the background may be unevenly woven with slubs in it or evenly woven and smooth. Coarse hessian, woollens, scrims or linens or other types down to fine muslins, canvas and nets are suitable for repetitive patterns and give a guide for

this sort of stitchery in which designs are built up either from pre-planned pattern or as the work progresses. To commence, add to the fabric rather than withdraw threads from it. This may be done by darning, drawn fabric work, canvas stitchery, blackwork or net embroidery, some of these types being reversible when embroidered, as is cross stitch if worked in a particular way. Look at the illustrations to see some of the ideas possible. Threads may be pulled together in bunches leaving holes as in drawn fabric work where a lacy effect is obtained if using a fine background such as handkerchief lawn but if hessian is the background fabric chosen, a bolder scale with a chunky surface suitable for wall decoration results. Eyelet holes and open stitches used together, with satin stitches and other solid surface ones, increase the variation in texture which can be very exciting if the right stitches are combined. It is possible to obtain (from furnishing departments of some stores) materials with woven stripes in which some of the warp threads have been omitted at intervals or very few are used, giving an open weave consisting mainly of the weft threads. These fabrics have innumerable possibilities for pulled work, weaving in patterns in contrasting colours and textures tying threads together, making holes and threading in beads, taking out threads, and generally experimenting. Threads, either warp or weft or both may be withdrawn from parts of evenly woven materials, leaving bands of vertical or horizontal threads and small open squares which are re-woven with patterns and colours as in needle-weaving, or they are tied and twisted into lace-like structures of openwork as in drawn thread and Italian cut work. Several techniques may be combined and on a simple scale much of this counted thread embroidery may be worked without too much planning on paper. The more advanced and intricate patterns may be worked out on squared graph paper if complete designs and exact stitchery are required before the work commences, but the whole field of embroidery in which the structure of the fabric is altered is vast and with exciting possibilities for development. See pages 17, 20 and 179.

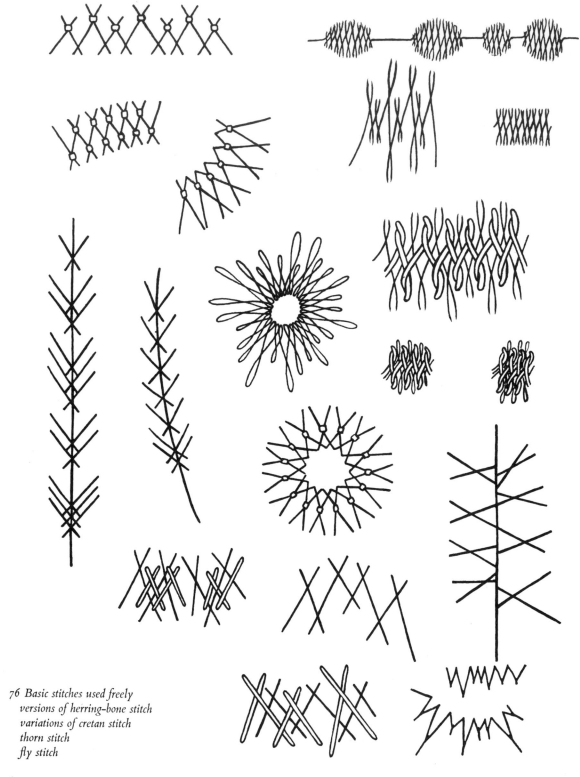

76 Basic stitches used freely
  versions of herring-bone stitch
  variations of cretan stitch
  thorn stitch
  fly stitch

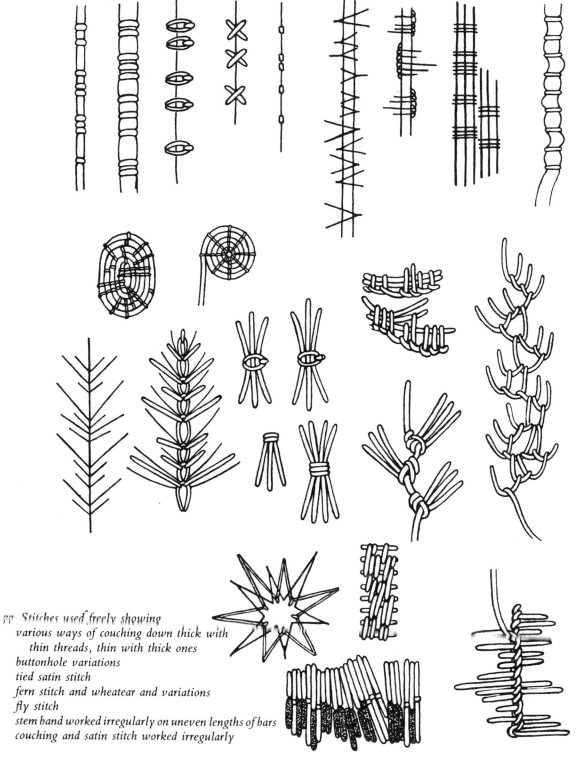

Stitches used freely showing
   various ways of couching down thick with
      thin threads, thin with thick ones
   buttonhole variations
   tied satin stitch
   fern stitch and wheatear and variations
   fly stitch
   stem band worked irregularly on uneven lengths of bars
   couching and satin stitch worked irregularly

65

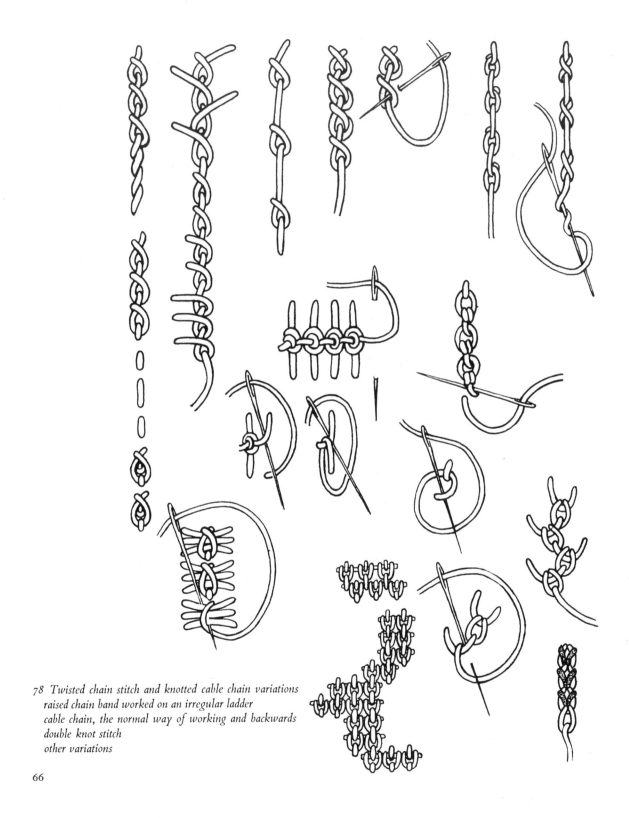

78 Twisted chain stitch and knotted cable chain variations
   raised chain band worked on an irregular ladder
   cable chain, the normal way of working and backwards
   double knot stitch
   other variations

79 *Variations on an embroidered spot pattern—half-penny to half-crown sized spots*

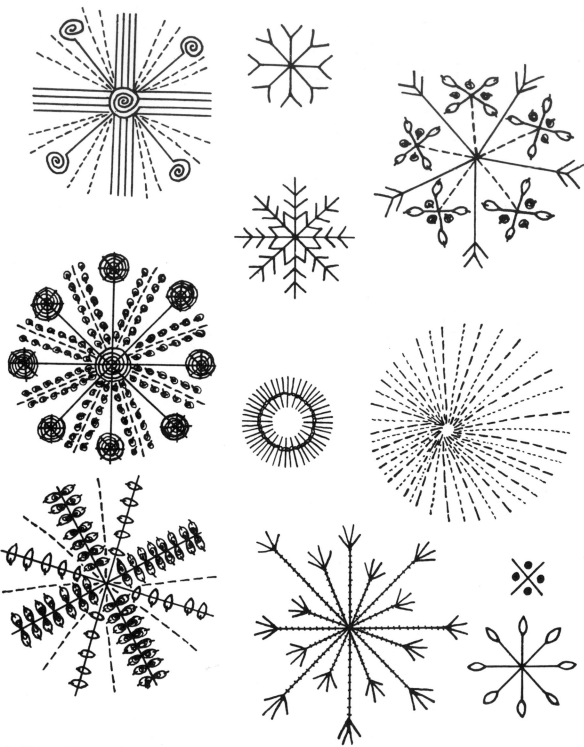

80 More variations on a larger spot pattern

81 Buttonhole and feather stitches giving a solid, textured appearance Lynn Jones

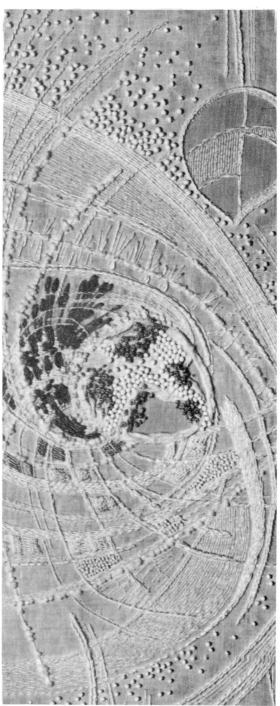

Geometric basis Shape is fundamentally geometric and built up from the straight or the curved line or both combined. It may be regular or irregular, repetitive or non-repetitive.

The pattern may be very simple or very complicated and as all design must have a plan it is advantageous to analyse other ways in which it may be developed beyond that of the fabric.

82 Thick threads used on organdie to give a rich effect. White anchor soft cotton, stranded cotton and beads, with slight changes of colour in grey and natural Ioné Dorrington

83 Uneven spots in both size, distribution and tone values. A sampler preceding the embroidering of a skirt on a similar material *Beryl Carter*

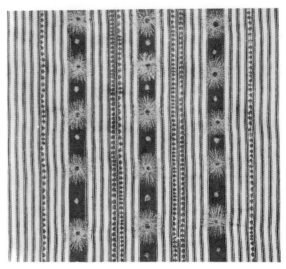

85 Ribbon stripes applied to emphasize those of the fabric, further embellished with machine embroidered spots *Christine Risley*

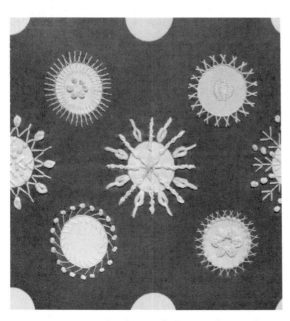

84 Spot patterns, embroidery worked on evenly spaced spots *Kaye Norris*

86 A spot pattern much enlarged showing french knots and and free stitchery

87 A spot pattern enlarged showing twisted chain whirls

89 A drawn fabric background with darned pattern to make the letter O   *Eirian Short*

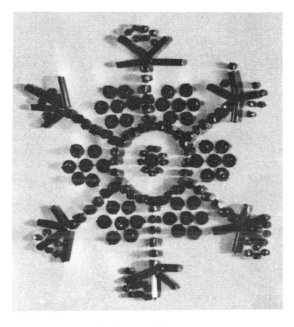

88 A spot pattern built up with beads

90 Needleweaving on the warp threads of linen. The weft is removed. The solid pattern is blocked in on the rough sketch, also the distribution of the main spaces as these versus the woven shapes give the vitality to the design. The contrast in areas, large against small shapes, solid against open must create the right balance to avoid monotony   *Ioné Dorrington*

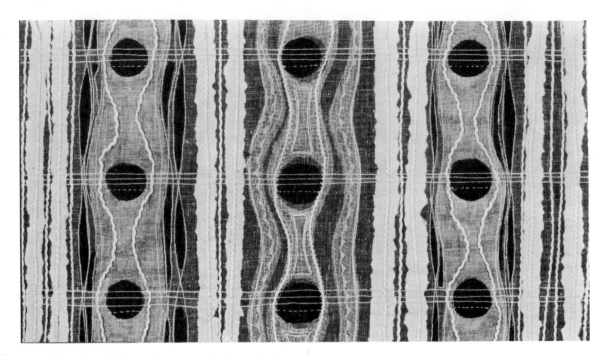

91 Cable stitch and free machinery combined, appliqué in tarletan and cotton on a black background   Mary Gwatkin Trent Park College of Education

The line   A line may be straight or curved, angular, wavy, thick, thin, broken or continuous, or a combination of these qualities. Embroidery may be interpreted entirely in line as distinct from shape and mass. Lines may be parallel as in stripes and plaids, arranged as grids of squares or in other geometric shapes such as hexagons and octagons, diamonds, bricks or lozenges non-parallel and in uneven grids; on these, patterns are planned for repetition or as complete units. These lines may be spaced evenly, irregularly, close together or far apart, of unequal lengths and variable in thickness, but as a method of regular repetition must be accurate, with equal spacing.

92 The line. Proportionate spacing, curves and zigzags. Grids and line directions, which give violent or gentle movement

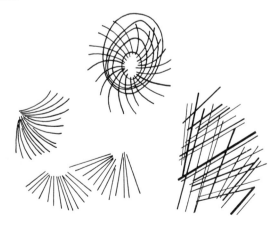

Exercise Use match sticks, drinking straws, string and other threads and thin paper strips, move these aids around on a background trying as many different arrangements of straight lines as possible, placing groups closely together, far apart, equally spaced and crossing over one another, unequal and crossing, watching the shapes between the lines. Soft threads will make good pliable curves, string, strong springy ones, combine curves and straight lines, make designs entirely in curves, in fact try as many arrangements as can be thought of in the time available. Lay straight line patterns in threads on a board fixed with nails or pins at certain intervals (see page 25 and figs 30 and 31). By passing the threads round pins and back to other pins interesting arrangements of both lines and shapes within the lines may be made. Again the variations are infinite, but the relationship of these shapes which will all be straight sided may be judged and if they are too equal or too variable the threads can be removed and replaced many times as the first arrangement will not necessarily be good. When interesting thread patterns are made (perhaps using more than one thread and in different colours and thicknesses) the ideas could be put down with coloured pencils on paper for future use drawing them from the patterns evolved by winding over the nails.

Shapes could be blocked in, between the lines, perhaps with pencil or coloured paper so that it would make the proportions more obvious, at the same time a different design would be evolving with line plus shape. Scrolls, whirls, spirals and

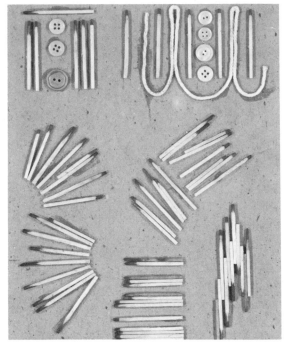

94 *Match sticks, buttons, threads, etc., used for spacing out preliminary patterns*

93 *Scrolls, spirals and twists using a variety of strings and cords*

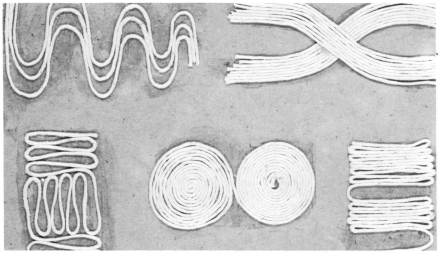

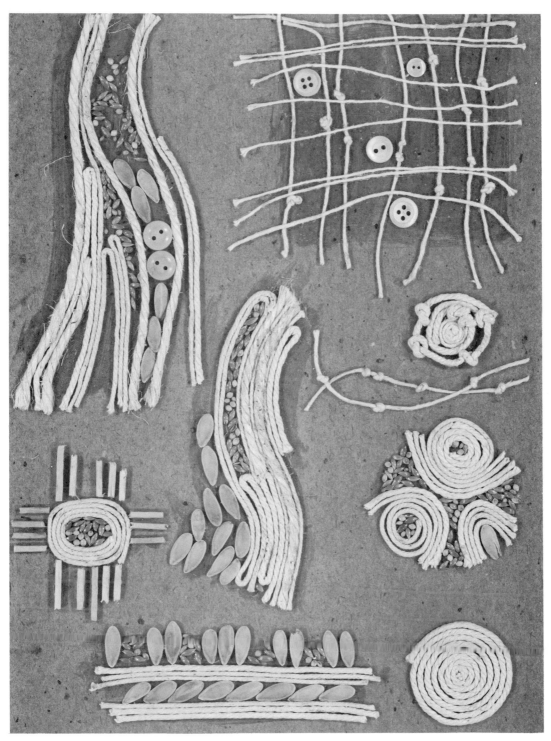

95 *String used to demonstrate the line and its variations. Various thicknesses of string spaced openly and closely,* *straight lines and curved lines. These exercises are translatable into embroidery*

twists are more easily manipulated with a soft string than by drawing, but any ways of producing straight and curved line designs are legitimate; rulers and compasses, drawing round curved shapes, using cords, braids and ribbons are all helpful as spacing is more easily arranged if the lines are movable and can be altered when wrong. Direction of line gives movement, such as shallow curved ones a gentle undulation, collections of jagged straight ones fierceness; their rhythm may be inward or outward, up or down, violent or calm, lines conforming in one direction give strength, those haphazardly scattered, diffusion of purpose and lack of rhythm.

Exercises Using strings of different thicknesses work out straight line patterns and stick them down on to a piece of cardboard, then work out some entirely composed of curves, then some in which curved and straight lines are combined, some having lines adjacent, some with spaces between them. Stick all the patterns down for reference then work similar arrangements in hand embroidery in a variety of stitches and threads, then again on a machine using cable stitch and free machining. Combine hand and machine embroidery and note how many variations may be obtained from these apparently simple exercises. Grasses with straight stems and heavily stitched heads are another idea using straight lines, which could be tried out after pure line patterns, the spacing between the stems and their lengths being varied to avoid monotony.

Proportion From these exercises it will be seen that design is greatly a matter of proportion and contrast. The thick line in conjunction with the thin is more interesting than two thin ones of equal length and width placed parallel to each other, a number grouped irregularly looks better than the same number placed at regular intervals over a surface, unless the spacing is deliberate and for a particular purpose when it is right. A balance of proportion applies to all design, equal spacing of equal units with similarly proportioned spaces in between is monotonous compared with unequal spacing, but if the units are all dissimilar and spaced irregularly the result is often restless and equal spacing would then be an asset.

Shape

The square By joining lines mass is achieved; geometric shapes are again a good beginning for design and the square and the rectangle are familiar shapes with infinite uses. They may be increased in breadth mathematically and proportionately well, using the radius of the diagonal for this alteration of area. To begin playing with squares, cut out equal sized ones, arrange them in a row equally apart, arrange them again and vary the spacing, see which is more interesting. Cut the squares into smaller squares and rectangles and re-arrange them. Cut a large square at random into shapes, spread out and re-arrange the pieces. Cut off the corners of the squares and rectangles so that they look smoother, re-arrange them—they can look like stones and pebbles. Combine small and large squares, rectangles and squares, lines and solid masses. By this playing around it is easily seen which arrangements are pleasant and which are not. The next step is to translate some of these arrangements into embroidery, working some shapes in solid stitchery some in line. The interpretation of these ideas should be individual but in accordance with purpose, and consequently scale. Colour and tone will add vitality and variation in texture and a semblance of depth. From this experiment many more ideas should develop. It is possible to cut a number of shapes, starting with a square, cutting off the corners and smoothing the straight edges until a circle evolves. A series of these shapes makes good pattern.

96 The square
  Increased in width by mathematical proportions. The radius of the diagonal gives the next width
  Squares spaced equally and unequally
  The square cut into squares and rectangles, also divided into squares and rectangles
  Embroidered squares using satin stitch and couching
  Stitches formed as squares
  Fabric cut diagonally and joined. Other diagrams show ideas for using the square

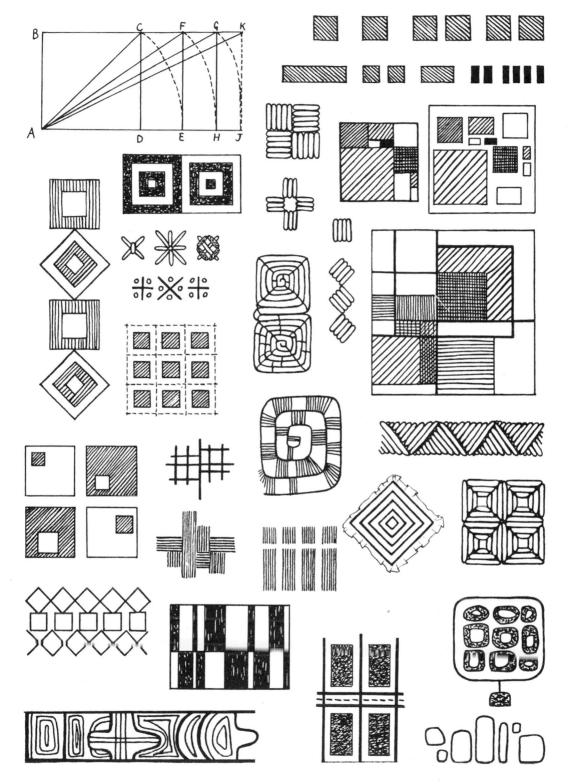

97 A band in felt, the open squares being filled with brightly coloured satins, the whole mounted on ribbon and stitched into place. This shows negative shapes. The positive shapes, left, show the squares cut out from the felt, placed together to make oblongs joined with lines of stitchery, all mounted on white petersham ribbon

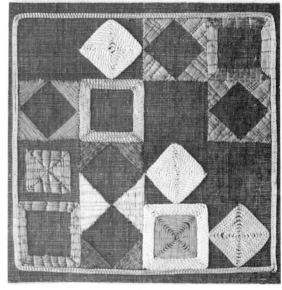

98 A panel based on squares and rectangles with the corners rounded. The embroidery is a combination of hand and machine stitchery with a variety of textures applied in black materials on a white ground　　　　　Ann Spence

99 A burse, the design evolved entirely from squares. The interest is in the method of couching down cords, metal threads and silks. The direction of threads gives light and shade and the omission of squares and parts of squares by leaving blank shapes, entirely alters the original grid pattern　　　　　Josephine Windebank

100 A cross composed of rectangles, worked in thick hand stitchery to give a rich textural quality   *Lynn Jones*

102 Patchwork border composed of squares, some embroidered
Josephine Canty

103 *Patchwork templates*

101 A large flower head, based on a square, built up with smaller squares, beads, thick and fine coloured threads on cream wool. A solid chunky effect is created by the overlaying of threads and stitches   *Brenda Holmes*

The circle   Circular and curved shapes may be used for experiment in a similar manner. The circle and square combined, of equal size or of unequal size will give many pattern variations. See how many can be thought of and alter the scale making some patterns very fine, some large and bold. Work some of them in applique, some in outline some in solid stitchery, as small samplers, before planning large-scale designs to be embroidered. Cut the circle into semi-circles and see what can be done both with outline embroidery and solid shapes, try using variously proportioned segments together, overlapping them, using them parallel to one another and generally playing around with them to find the most interesting combinations of shapes.

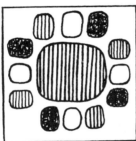

105 *A cushion cover in cream wools on a cream woollen background. The circle is about 8 inches in diameter and gives a raised effect* Sheila Beattie

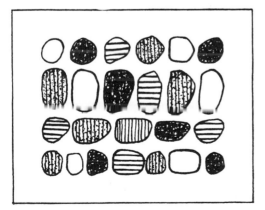

104 *The circle*
combined with the square
semi-circles
circles cut up
segments of circles
shapes derived from rectangles with corners rounded
a cross between circles and squares
Other ideas for breaking up and using a number of circles

106 Two jars, covered with embroidered felt. The patterns on the lids fit the simple circular shapes, embellished with beads and sequins
Anne Preston

Exercise The square and circle may both be built up entirely in stitchery from a central spot, working outwards without previous planning, starting centrally, building up stitches in both thick and thin threads, knobbly, flat and open stitches, expanding from the spot to a larger motif (4 to 6 inches in diameter) approximately or according to the scale required. Use a contrasting colour or self colour for the embroidery so that textures may be more varied without too much colour to confuse them. When these exercises are finished move the spot off centre in the circle and work another motif, increasing the stitchery in weight, on one side, lessening it on the other. The result will be more interesting and quite different. Patterns may be built up entirely in small mosaic like spots of squares and circles. Felt and stitchery combined are suitable for this, the shapes being similar in size but different in colour and texture, or dissimilar in size although

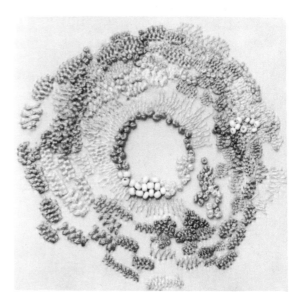

107 A motif for dress embroidery, with a non-symmetrical arrangement of cretan stitch spots, french knots and beads. Worked in a variety of threads within a circular shape
Josephine Canty

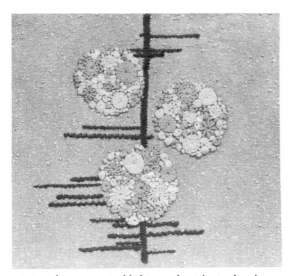

108 A cushion cover in khaki tweed, with circular shapes worked in mosaic-like stitching of pinks, oranges and reds
Theckla Finck

110 A motif for dress based on a circle, using beads, sequins and stitchery

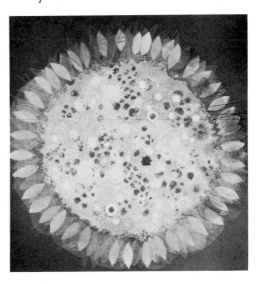

109 A very simple, circular motif using beads, sequins and stitchery

111 A large sunflower head 36 inches square, using a mosaic-like combination of hand and machine embroidery. Overlaid nets are cut away to the background in sections, with spaces filled in with hand stitchery   Margaret Maugham

still small, of one colour and varied textures. Beads, sequins and French knots could be built up into rich jewel-like motifs, worked out on this principle. Pincushions with pinheads, beads and sequins would make amusing exercises for pattern too. This idea could relate to the working of parts of enlarged centres of flower heads and collections of stones and pebbles, embroidered as textured backgrounds to complement larger shapes.

Try similar experiments with other geometric shapes, the triangle and diamond, vary both proportions and combinations of these shapes, cut them in coloured tissue papers, again overlap similar or different shapes to produce third shapes which will develop into more complicated designs. Nets and organdie could be used in embroidery for this exercise.

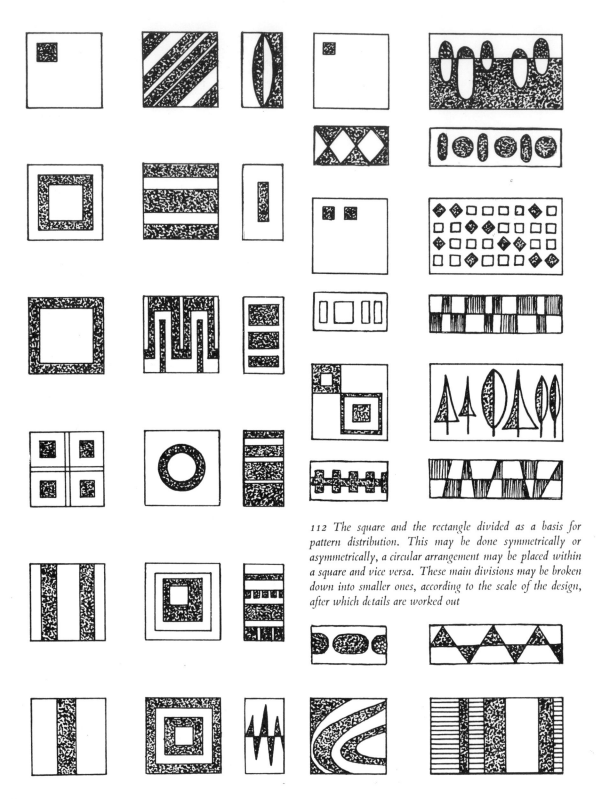

112 *The square and the rectangle divided as a basis for pattern distribution. This may be done symmetrically or asymmetrically, a circular arrangement may be placed within a square and vice versa. These main divisions may be broken down into smaller ones, according to the scale of the design, after which details are worked out*

113 Distribution of pattern within the circle and the semi-circle. These lines and areas give only the main direction of movement on which pattern is built up from the broad basis to the fine detail

114 *Triangles and diamonds as a basis for design. Over-lapping with transparent fabrics gives interesting result*

115 *The ends of a stole, consisting of diamonds embroidered in laid work, in graduated colours, overlaid with couched gold threads*
Flora Walton

116 *The triangle and diamond as ideas for patchwork*

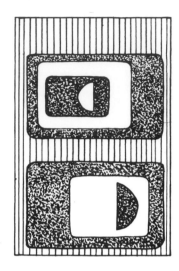

117 The arrangement of similar units within differently proportioned areas

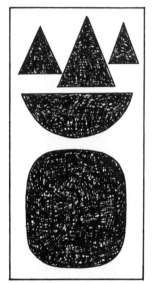

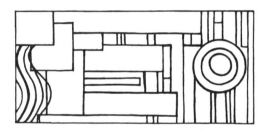

118 The same shapes, differently proportioned placed within an area; suitable for a variety of purposes

119 (a) A rectangle divided into a number of much smaller shapes
(b) a circle divided within a square

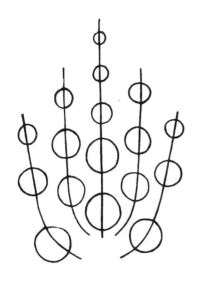

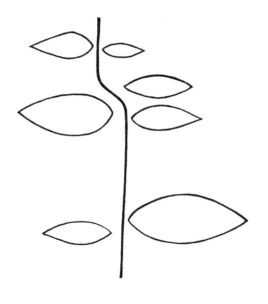

120 *The repetition of a similar shape but of different proportions*

121 *A felt tea cosy embroidered on the machine*
  'Day' depicting the sun
  the reverse side of the tea cosy showing 'Night' with the moon and clouds
  In each, the circle is the basis of the design, round which other pattern is built up. Worked in a number of colours
                                        Phyllis Hallett

Buildings Following on from the use of geometric shapes which can be planned and arranged in innumerable permutations, study from reality is the next step from which ideas are obtained. With a geometric basis as a beginning again, buildings are a simple and obvious answer as the starting point. They are generally made up of cubes, cylinders, or solid rectangular and often triangular shapes with curves in the architectural details, requiring little alteration except in dimension for flat decoration. In basing designs on reality any of the shapes may be re-distributed, their proportions changed and any parts not wanted eliminated. By cutting out in variously toned papers a number of rectangles and squares in different sizes, almost any buildings could be constructed from these shapes into designs, with arrangements for windows, doors, roofs, or ornament.

The main point of interest in any design other than the subject matter, colour, tone and texture, is in the relationship of the shapes to one another and their arrangement within a given area, such as within a narrow, horizontal panel, a square or vertical panel or an irregular one, or a circle as the shape and proportions of background area dictate those to be enclosed. Individual details of decoration, surface qualities and variety of textures are obtained by choice of background materials, threads and techniques, and the interpretation in stitchery suitable to these. Any features in reality which do not help the design should be omitted and although it is often difficult to determine which these are at first, the elimination of unnecessary ones is more easily decided as further design is practised and understood.

122 Simple architectural units for design

123 A panel of three equally-sized circular shapes, each different in treatment but related in weight of stitchery and proportion of bands. Cream on a cream woollen ground. The circles are approximately 14 inches in diameter

Sheila Beattie

Emphasis The designer must learn to make a personal selection from the reality which has given the initial inspiration for the idea. It is impossible to include everything in a flat decoration and all design is a matter of selection and elimination, rather a breaking down into simplicity before the re-construction begins. Unnecessary details and those of no particular interest should be omitted so that the 'bare bones' are left. When this stage is reached the re-building and original creative outlook takes over. As everyone is an individual with a different viewpoint, so each will find a different point of interest from which to develop the idea, and although these may be taken from a common source the results will be dissimilar and all will show an exaggeration or emphasis of a different feature. In this way design keeps lively and originality of outlook being one of the main assets it is worth trying to preserve a freshness of vision in approaching any problem.

Concentrated observation of detail is another means by which ideas are fostered, as when these are understood they may be enlarged considerably to make complete designs; in fact, detail increased many times its natural size in scale is a source of much exciting pattern of today. The joint of a main and subsidiary stem of any plant, enlarged from one inch to one foot, could make a design for a panel or a cushion cover, often with little alteration. A thorny stem could be enlarged as an idea for a heavy border motif on a curtain, or might be the idea from which a pattern on a net curtain is worked. A thumb print in ink on paper could be enlarged sufficiently to be made into a design for a large wall hanging in which texture predominates. With this enlarging of detail a camera would be of value with photographs 'blown up' to the required size, and, plus drawings there would be an accurate record to supplement them for the working out of ideas. Before a photograph is taken study of the details selected should be made from all angles, with preliminary normal sized drawings which are enlarged afterwards, when a final decision has been made on the requirements of the design. This selective method of drawing requires effort and practice but will lead to considerable improvement in ability to choose and to draw for a purpose and consequently to design.

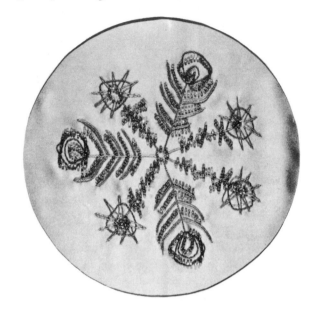

124 *Two motifs worked from the same design*
(a) *using beads and threads on satin for dress embroidery*
(b) *on organdie, entirely worked in stitchery, for a circular mat. This is a spot pattern the size of a dinner plate*
Kaye Norris

125 A panel, although abstract, based on the circle. Appliqué in a variety of materials   *Janet Graham*

127 A border for dress in machine embroidery. A double layer of organdie is stitched round the pattern shapes, one layer is cut away and in some parts both layers. A simple diamond motif which could be very much elaborated as required

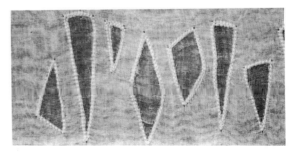

126 A panel based on a circular shape, floral or geometric in inspiration   *Cynthia Sharpe*

128 Triangles 'arranged' haphazardly for dress decoration, single on double organdie, machine embroidery which could be developed into heavier decoration

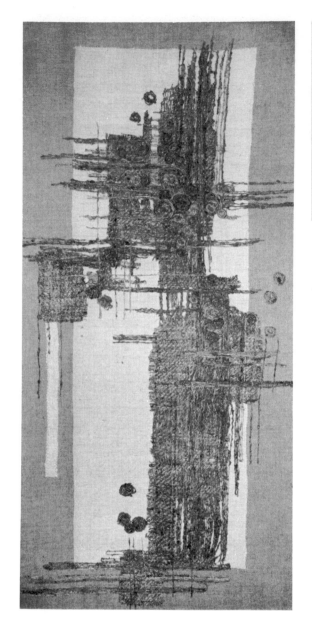

130 (a) *Two simple blackwork buildings with a balanced distribution of lines. The omission of outlines gives more freedom to this traditional embroidery* Muriel Swift

129 *A panel—green blue silk tweed on cream silk tweed. Some of the threads have been pulled out of the green tweed and used in raised circles to give a three-dimensional effect. The idea is based on building construction with scaffolding* Molly Arnold

130 (b) *A tower in blackwork, an elementary shape based on the rectangle*

131 A richly ornamented building, composed of rectangles and curved shapes. Appliqué and beads with some stitchery
Kaye Norris

132 A group of buildings in hardanger work, with various stitches   Sunderland College of Education

133 A simple house based on reality. Several houses have been drawn and some of their features combined in this panel
Iris Cox

Natural form All design has a basic structure from which it grows; from a central spot expanding outwards, from a base extending upwards or downwards, horizontally to right or left or diagonally. It may be symmetrical in balance or asymmetrical but must have a focal point or area of dominant interest. This may be achieved by shape, colour and tone or by contrasting textures. Shape may be emphasized by the repetition of line or mass, and most design may be planned geometrically whatever the original source of ideas. As natural form is reducible to geometric shapes, this is a good method of simplification in the initial stages, in working from reality to flat pattern.

Some natural form is simple and well balanced and requires little alteration to conventionalize it, but usually there must be replanning of shapes, elimination of the third dimension and accidental details, and emphasis of particular characteristics of growth to consider. This last feature is important as if it is ignored much of the vigour and attraction of the plant is lost in the design. The general structure and individual quality of this growth and its direction may be rigid and stiff or flowing and tangled, it may be strong or delicate and some of this character must be retained in the design if it is to have meaning.

Details of natural forms may be studied, enlarged and embroidered as samplers, choosing those parts which appeal for their shapes or textures, such as knots in woody stems, veining in stones, patterns on feathers, thorns and spikey protuberances, fine and fluffy seeds or hard scaly ones. Before planning any design draw or cut out in paper those things which have a personal interest. Study the chosen subject carefully, and try to analyse the quality of its attraction, whether its shape, texture or colour give most interest, as this is the beginning of individual interpretation, and is the point from which art develops as without personal feelings there can be no creative urge.

A sketch book is valuable at this stage as all these observations can be recorded, paper shapes being stuck in the book, sketches drawn and notes made on colour and particular aspects found by this approach.

Translation to pattern From this study the most exciting but difficult part, the making of the design commences. Certain questions must now be asked and answered. What is the purpose of the design? Is it to be a complete unit for a given shape, or a repetitive unit and if the latter, a spot pattern or a continuous one, a border or an all-over pattern?

When these questions are settled rough ideas should be tried out before the final design is decided upon, therefore the scale in the beginning may not be absolutely accurate. In the finished work proportionately accurate measurements must be made as the amount of detail shown in the finished drawing depends upon this scale. On the other hand the size of a natural form may be considerably enlarged or reduced to fit a given shape. A daisy may be 3 feet in diameter or 3 inches, a tree may be 6 inches high or 6 feet high, according to the final purpose of the design.

Eliminate true perspective and from the rough plans decide whether the whole form or part of the form is to be used as the main idea, whether front and side views might be used concurrently as flat pattern, whether profile or front views of birds, animals or human figures are more suitable for the purpose in mind or if both views could be combined successfully. It is only by trying out these alternatives that a satisfactory result is derived. By cutting the initial ideas in paper, which tends to simplification, automatically some of the difficulties solve themselves.

A decision must be made on the focal point of the design, what features are to be emphasized and how this is best done. Try out different arrangements of the cut paper shapes, in different proportions, e.g. in one pattern emphasize the leaves of a plant as the basis for design, in another concentrate on making the flower the focal point, working from the same subject. Shift things around within a given area and if no arrangements look right, start again. These preliminary trial and error tactics must be pursued if the most satisfactory results are to be achieved. It is only by constant practice that the eye can learn to discriminate between the good and not so good, the well planned and the poorly spaced.

'Blue Moon' 3ft square appliqué in silks, velvets and organza. One crescent shape has been used for the entire design, cutting it smaller as the pattern is built up. Beads and raised stitchery complete the embroidery

Constance Howard

Machine embroidery: an exercise in the use of pure hues
Sister Marie Louie

Plant form is one of the most extensive sources of inspiration for design and is particularly suitable as a source of ideas for embroidery design. A danger is that it is easily imitable in stitchery, an effect of reality being obtained with shading in long and short stitch. This realistic copying is not design and is to be avoided. Remember the idea of reducing natural to geometric shapes, for with plant form this is an excellent way of simplication.

Exercises Take some flowering grasses, arrange them together on a background until they appear well spaced. Try to define their characteristics, such as those with heavy heads, fine stiff stalks, fluffy heads, wiry stems, closed shapes such as corn, open ones such as quaking grass. Each head is composed of smaller shapes but try to see as well the simple overall appearances of the different grasses. The heads may be represented by cut paper shapes, the stems by string in the initial stage of designing. Grasses may be embroidered as samplers in which several versions of each kind are worked differently, the most successful of each type being chosen for a final design which contains various grasses. By different combinations of threads and stitches a great variety of interesting grassy textures is possible.

Leaves In order to use plants for inspiration it is a good idea to take parts of them and study these before attempting to design from whole plants. As a beginning leaves are a good point of departure and have enormous variety in size, shape and colour, also in pattern and vein structure. Their edges may be smooth, serrated, indented or wrinkled, they may have shiny, dull or hairy surfaces. The complete leaves may consist of many smaller leaflets growing on subsidiary stems, they may have dark upper surfaces with pale under sides or may be variegated, spotted or striped. The arrangements of growth may be in opposite pairs on a main stem, alternate or irregular, or they may grow quite separately on subsidiary stems of their own which join at the bases of the plants. Many more features are listable but it is possible to find an enormous variety throughout the natural world in a greater or lesser degree. If this attitude of enquiry into the study of leaves is extended to other things an

enormous fund of information will be built up; also an acute observation. Having discovered the fascination of leaves they may now be used as a basis for working out whole designs starting with contrasting shapes. By working in stitchery, sometimes in outline, sometimes solidly, sometimes as appliqué, an infinite number of interesting arrangements for many different purposes is possible, based entirely on leaf shapes.

Stems and trunks, bare branches and twigs are another source of ideas for design. They have completely different characteristics from leaves, with different surfaces and are ideal for a basis of linear arrangements of pattern and areas of solid stitchery.

The textures on the stems and trunks, smooth, bumpy, ridged and knobbly, prickly or hairy are translatable into interesting embroidered patterns and the intricate interlacing of branches and stems when leafless, are exciting in every way. There are too many branches in many cases and here selection of the important ones must be made. Some may have to be re-spaced and some of them removed for good two dimensional results, but both the branches and the spaces between those branches are suitable as patterns, the positive and negative shapes may have equal possibilities according to whether patterns in line or mass are to be designed (see figs 28, 29 and 46).

Flowers and flower clusters should be studied as separate entities before combining them with the rest of the plants. They again have infinite variety from three petalled arrowhead to multi-petalled chrysanthemums, from one flower to a composite cluster of florets such as cow parsley or lilac. Many heads are symmetrical with petals radiating from a central point, such as the daisy, from the small wild one to the huge sunflower. Other heads are composed of clusters of florets which give the appearance of solid shapes and may be worked as embroidery, in detail or as simple mass, the onion flower head, lupins, cow parsley and hyacinths are in this group. Others grow as bells, such as the harebell and foxglove, some are so multi-petalled that it it difficult to define the essential qualities from which designs could be developed. Sometimes the stamens are a basis for

97

134 An espalier, worked in a variety of natural and cream threads, wooden button moulds, beads and string   Iris Cox

135 A detail of the espalier showing a knotty trunk, with an interesting mixture of textures used together

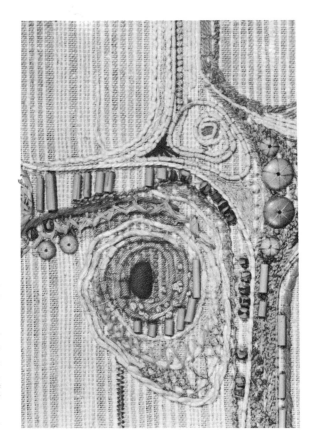

pattern, being prominent features of the flowers as in some lilies and fuchsias, in others the calyx is of most importance as in love-in-a-mist. It is obvious that some flower heads are more adaptable than others to flat pattern, some have features which make them suitable for considerable enlargement without the addition of stems and leaves. Here again use a magnifying glass for detail.

Exercise Take any symmetrically arranged flower head, study it carefully; are all the petals alike, is the centre wider in diameter than the length of petal, are there smaller petals near the centre, with larger ones behind them or is there a single layer of petals, are the stamens important, are they loose and pendulous or are they tightly packed together, how can the head successfully be adapted to embroidery, which parts of it should be emphasized? By asking these questions it is easier to decide which features are important as a basis on which to plan the pattern, but again according to purpose one feature might be better for one type of embroidery, another for a different technique. Try cutting out in paper in different sizes, shapes based on one flower and with emphasis on different features. Here it may be useful to have two colours of paper, one for the centre and even two for the petals. Cut a number of petals, equal and unequal in sizes. Put those of varied sizes together and those of a similar size together to see which looks better and is more suitable for its purpose. Move the point of interest from the symmetrical to the asymmetrical and work out in this way ideas from different flowers to see how the change in balance affects the appearance of the final pattern. See how many shapes and linear patterns can be extracted from one flower head. After this careful dissection, take more difficult and less obvious heads or clusters of florets and analyse them in a similar way, enlarging, emphasizing and extracting as much as possible from them. Designs of flower heads either used singly or grouped can be planned to fill large areas without the addition of stems and leaves—in fact they are often more exciting on their own.

Seed heads and pods are quite fascinating to study. They are excellent sources for design of any kind and the small seeds and the large cases in which they are contained are both superb in shapes and textures, being harder and more brittle compared with that of the flowers. Vegetables and fruits are in this area of study and are a wide source of inspiration. Draw them from different angles, cut them into transverse and longitudinal sections and make drawings of these: some will be found as almost perfect patterns without alteration. Parts can be enlarged such as the central core and pips in an apple, one scale of a pineapple, the texture of a cabbage leaf, the ring divisions seen in a carrot or turnip. In fact now that this breaking down and searching has become second nature everything will be seen with its possibilities as design for embroidery.

Having concentrated on different parts of plant form, attempts should then be made at design in which complete plants are used. This may be difficult but again the proportions of flowers to leaves, the height of the stem, the distribution of leaves and flowers in relation to this height and to one another, the general character of growth are the main points of departure. The simplification of the individual parts to suit the needs of the design, its scale and purpose is the ultimate aim in working out the idea. Trees and shrubs come into this category (see page 97) and the same approach in using them as a basis of design is applicable as it is to that of plant form generally. Branches may be bare, covered in leaves only or in leaves plus flowers, or fruits or all together. The trees may be planned as silhouettes without individual branches and leaves and are easily reduced to geometric forms for embroidery in outline or mass. Parts only may be used for design, such as the bark textures on the trunks, the boles and knots, or the interstices of trunks and branches. Certain parts might be emphasized. Take one tree and make the trunk and branches important, the foliage subsidiary; reverse the process and make the trunk of secondary importance, the leaves very large and the main features of the pattern. By this process it will be more easily seen which result is better for its purpose.

Roots of plants are quite beautiful and drawings from them are suitable for ideas using fine and lacy stitchery, wood grains have the same qualities, both would enlarge well for coarse wool embroidery as well as for the fine, lacy types.

The placing of a number of designed plants or trees together within a given area is still a matter of balance in proportion and contrast of shape, of pattern against background, of line against mass, of dark against light and this is best planned in cut paper before adding any details; whether it is a design for a small tray cloth or a large curtain for a stage, the principles are the same and if each part is worked out step by step based on the preceding suggestions, a reasonable result should be possible.

99

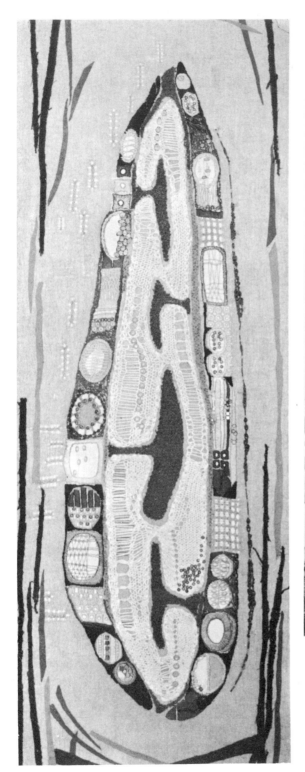

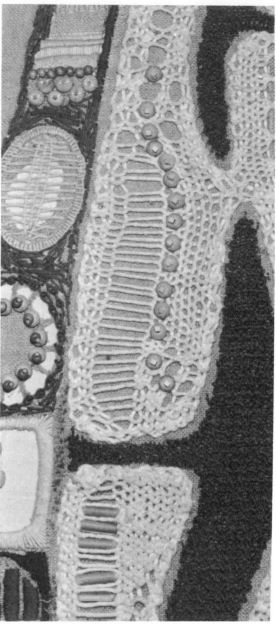

*136 A panel using wooden beads, knitting, various techniques,
based on a native shield
A detail of the panel*   *Audrey Stevens*

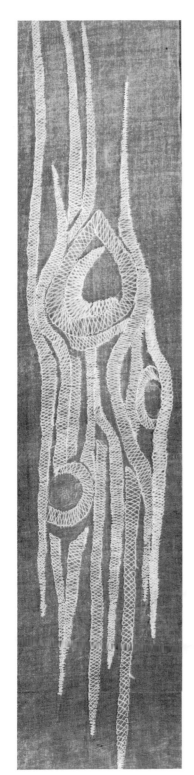

137 Various ways in which bark has been interpreted
shadow work
surface stitchery
beads and sequins   Cynthia Prentice

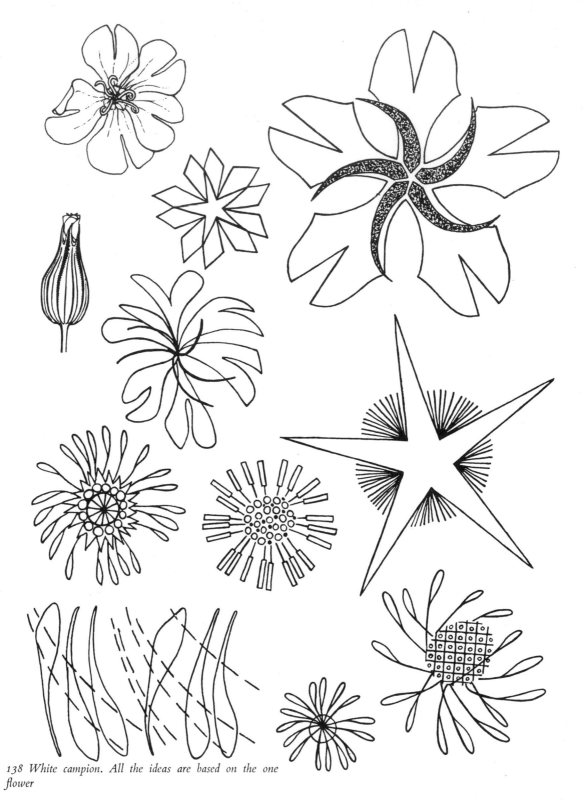

138 *White campion. All the ideas are based on the one flower*

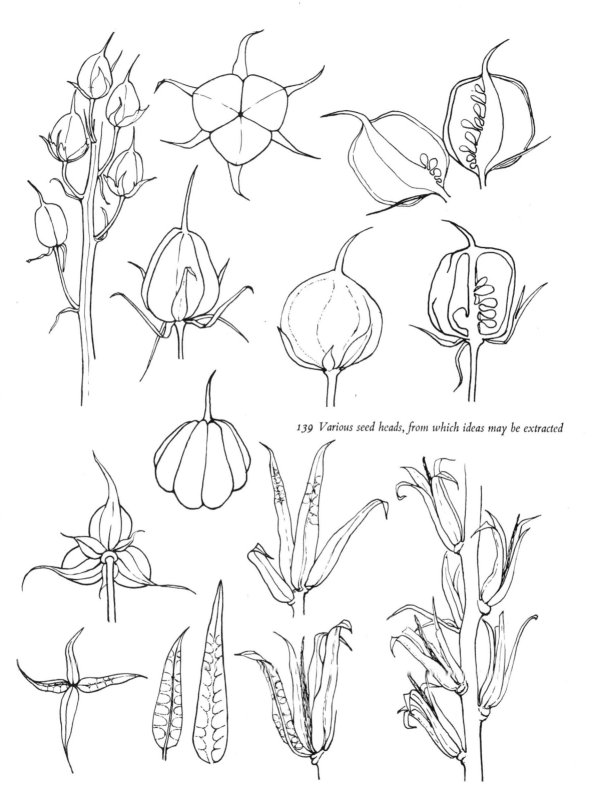

139 Various seed heads, from which ideas may be extracted

140 *A seed head cut longitudinally showing an idea for shadow work*

143 *A tray cloth in organdie embroidered with grasses. From whichever way the tray cloth is viewed, there is no right or wrong way of pattern*   Mary Honeywood

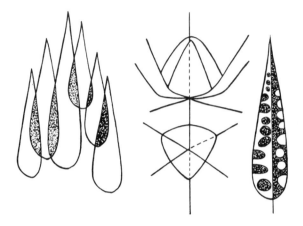

141 *Motifs based on drawings of seed heads*

142 *Grass from a shadow, embroidered directly on to the fabric*

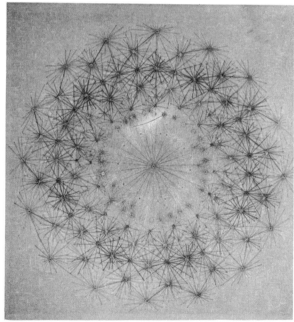

144 'Puffball'—*a delicate but large embroidery, approximately 3 feet square, based on a dandelion clock in which threads are raised over beads and are strung across to the next group of beads—in pale pinks, greys and white, in three layers*

145 *A detail*   Sister Marie Louie

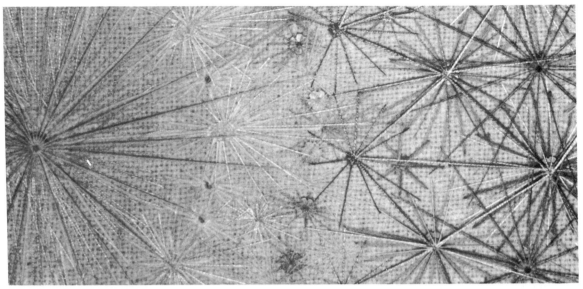

145

146 A sun-flower head embroidered in a variety of gold threads with string and felt padding and some gold kid appliqué also padded. The direction of laying the threads gives depth and tone to the work   *Molly Arnold*

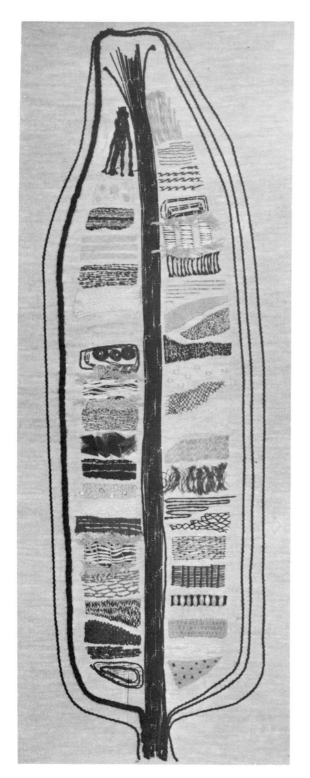

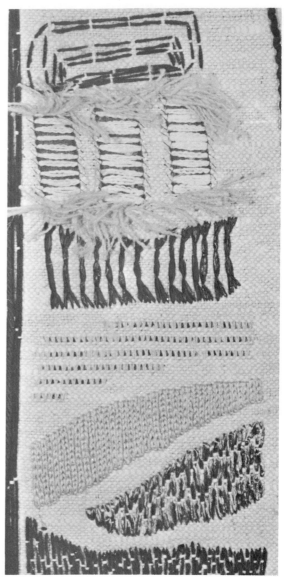

147 *A pepper worked as a sampler on a large scale about 3 feet 6 inches by 16 inches. Experiments using all kinds of threads and techniques have been incorporated in the shape which has a decorative value as well as a use as a sampler*

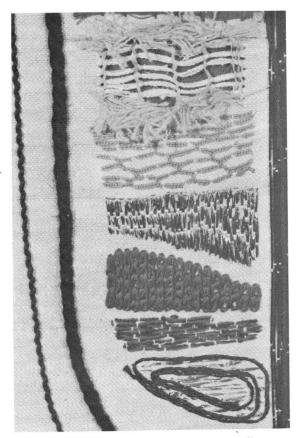

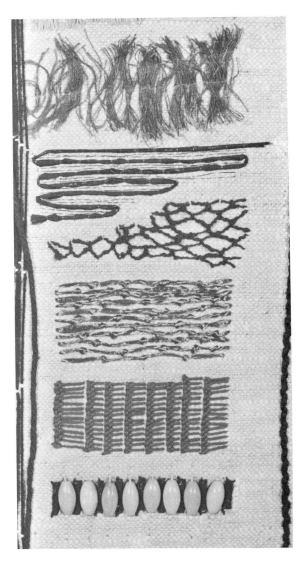

148 *Four details enlarged from the sampler showing a free use of techniques*   *Mary Stanley*
Avery Hill College of Education

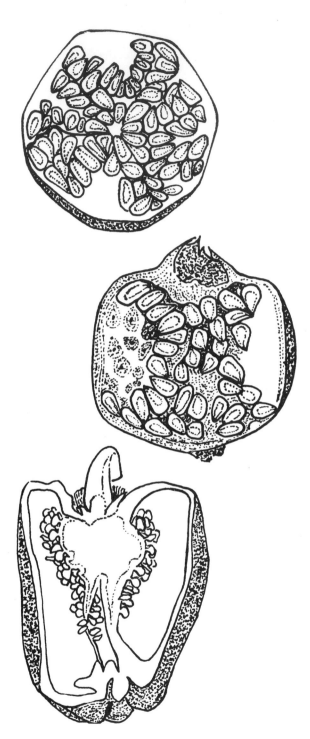

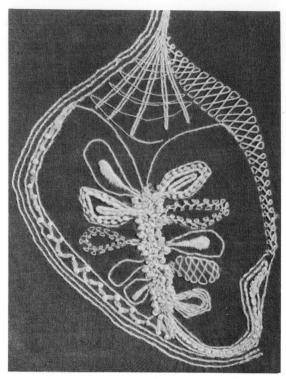

150 *A pepper embroidered in thick threads on organdie*
Josephine Canty

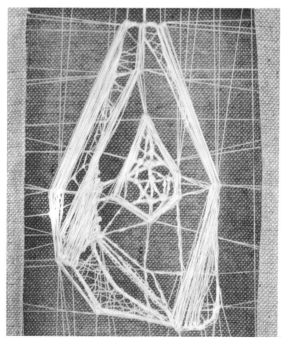

149 *Drawings of both transverse and longitudinal sections of fruit, pomegranates and a green pepper*

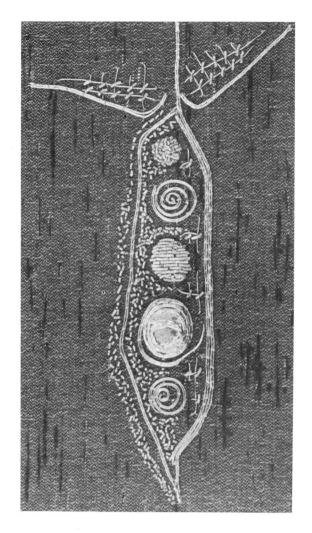

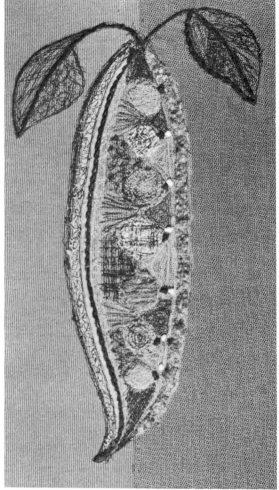

152 *A simple exercise in gold embroidery, the design based on a pod of peas* Muriel Swift

153 *A pod of peas worked in machine embroidery on the cover of a book* Janet Green
Avery Hill College of Education

151 *A construction based on a vertical section of a fruit. Part embroidery, part weaving* Doreen Welbourn
Avery Hill College of Education

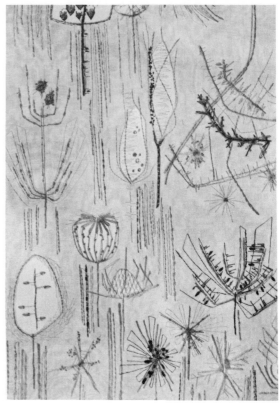

154 (a) *A panel of white organdie applied in several layers of fabric. A head surrounded with grasses and seed pods worked in free stitchery and shadow embroidery. White and neutral coloured threads are used in a variety of thicknesses and in parts some of the organdie is cut away to a single layer*

Ioné Dorrington

(b) *A detail showing some of the seed heads*

(c) *A detail of grasses*

155 *Trees and shrubs, reduced to geometric shapes, flattened and simplified with emphasis on certain features*

III

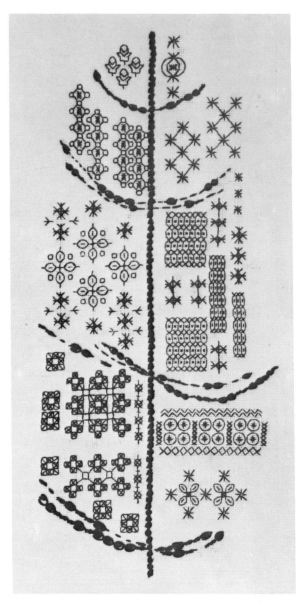

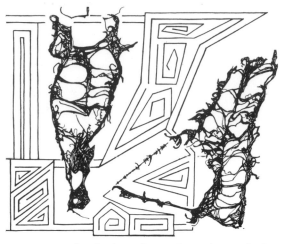

157 Drawing of a dried membrane of a melon, with the beginning of an idea for canvas embroidery roughed in. The membrane was pinned out to prevent shrinking and curling

156 A blackwork sampler built up from tree forms
Barbara Cooper

158 The final idea for the canvas embroidery drawn in greater detail

The embroidered canvas panel, with holes cut in it behind which stained glass and mirror glass is placed. Jewels are also incorporated. A variety of stitches is used in different thicknesses of thread Mary Rhodes

159 *Panel on white linen in black, bright blue and dull yellow. Sunflower and honesty seeds. Some parts are padded and various textures are used* Constance Howard

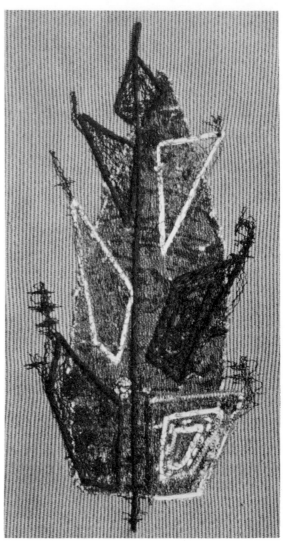

161 *Tree form in machine embroidery for a book cover*
Janet Green
Avery Hill College of Education

160 *Panel 'Figures in a wood', here the striped material dictated the idea. The trees and figures are reduced almost to silhouettes with textures to give depth to them. A variety of threads is used for the embroidery* Ioné Dorrington

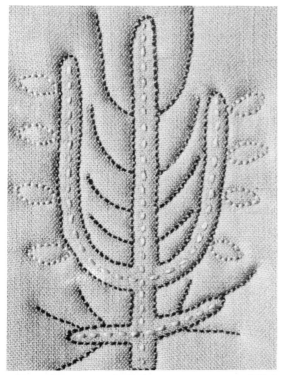

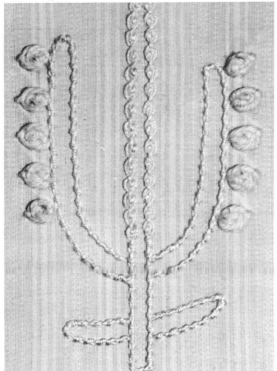

162 A series of simple tree shapes—alike except for minor details. Each is worked differently to show how the same basic shape may be altered by tone and by choice of stitches and threads

  quilting in dark and light coloured threads
  outline in twisted chain and knotted cable chain with
    detached knotted cable chain
  darning in outline on net using two thicknesses of thread
                                                Kaye Norris

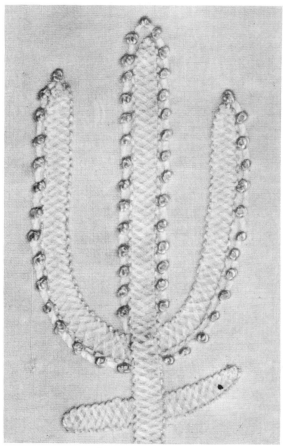

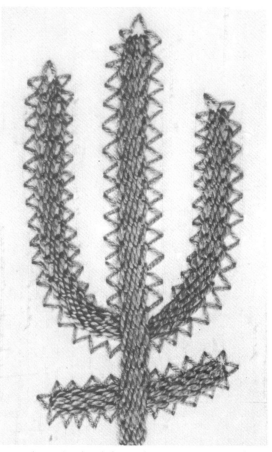

shadow work and french knots

raised stem band and fly stitch in perle to give a heavy appearance

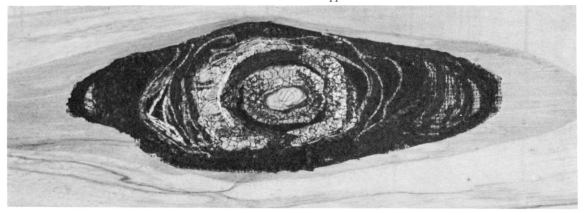

163 This idea results from finding a piece of discarded wood in the workshop. The knot has fallen out and an embroidered one is substituted. This is padded, worked with machine and hand embroidery, using browns, bronze and greenish colours. The finished work has a jewel-like quality. About 12 in. long

Marion Badley
Trent Park College of Education

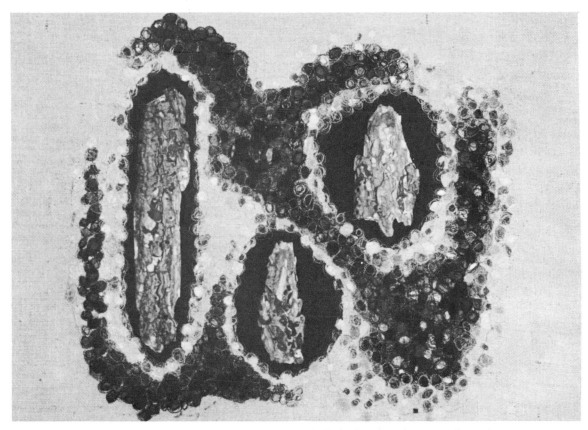

164 *Tree bark and seed pods incorporated in an embroidered panel. The textures of the machine embroidery echo those of the bark, the colours have a similar quality*

Marion Badley
Trent Park College of Education

Rocks, shells, stones and pebbles, rock strata and crystals seen with the naked eye or under a microscope have beautiful pattern, colour and texture, the smallest chips becoming jewel like when magnified. Some veining could be translated straight away to stitchery and some rock formations reduced to mosaic like textures. Study these in the same way as the plant form, cutting shapes in paper, eliminating those not wanted, but looking at them always from the point of view of flat and simplified pattern which is translatable into stitchery. Shells and spiral forms have infinite variety and can be used for design ideas both from the structural angle and the pattern and colour seen in them. Many have interesting surface qualities almost like stitchery, encrustations and wavy surfaces giving depths which are exciting and workable in threads of different thicknesses and would enlarge as designs for wall panels and hangings. Invent patterns based on these surfaces, see how many shapes may be taken from shells, both in line and mass and how many patterns may be used just as they are, or combined with variations invented from the natural ones. Emphasize some shapes, thicken some lines, break others down so that they hardly exist. Make very large patterns from the small natural forms. Make repeating patterns with small units from rock surfaces and shells, turn these upside down, sideways or rotate them, in fact do not be afraid to experiment all the time, as until a number of ideas have been carried out it is impossible to ascertain which is best for its purpose.

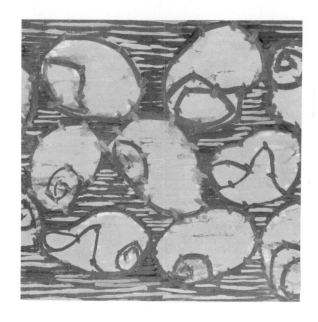

165 Shells as a basis of ideas—a freely painted sketch
Hilary Taylor

166 Gold couched threads, purl and silk. A line decoration
taken from shell patterns

167 Patterns based on shells
  sketch for striped pattern
  sketches for line embroidery freely painted
Hilary Taylor

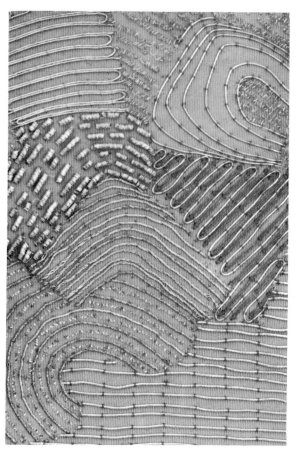

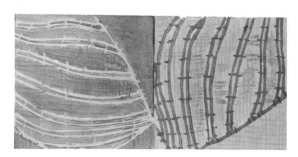

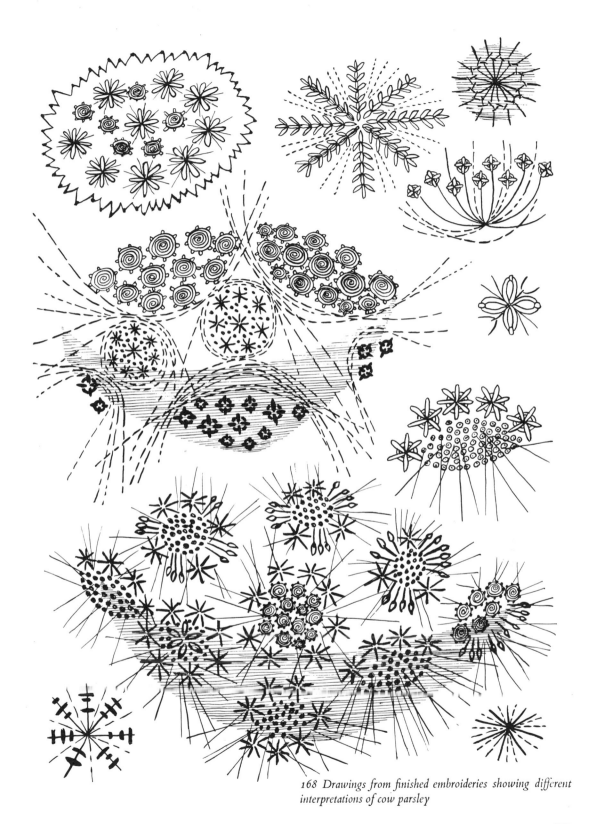

168 *Drawings from finished embroideries showing different interpretations of cow parsley*

Birds, animals, fishes, reptiles, insects To understand how moving things work and to determine their particular characteristics they must be observed for some length of time before attempting to draw them or cut out shapes in paper. After careful observation, whenever possible draw whatever provides most interest. Model it from reality in clay or any suitable medium as this gives an understanding of the whole form not possible in a drawing. Try to see the rhythm of the movement and the main structure of the creature being studied. Then attempt to draw from memory after drawing from life but from a different viewpoint. This will clarify points of importance in articulation, proportions and special features. If they cannot be remembered look again at reality. After successful drawings are made, cut out in paper similar shapes to those drawn, but with simplifications which are inevitable with this medium but are suitable for two dimensional design. Then simplify again for the final patterns.

In order to make most use of moving creatures when planning ideas for design constant looking is the only answer, then drawing from life and memory and a final reduction to two dimensional, simple, cut paper shapes until the results are almost geometric in idea. Most birds and animals have a sinuous quality in movement, their heads and bodies merge smoothly. Try to emphasize this in design as it is a source of vitality and gives co-ordination to the whole idea. When certain creatures are selected for design find out which features of theirs to enlarge to emphasize their main characteristics and which to modify. In designing with bird forms the placing of the legs in relation to the bodies can give a static or lively appearance. The sizes of heads in proportion to those of bodies and tails the lengths of necks, legs and tails, all in ratio to heads and bodies give completely different effects according to their combinations. Try drawing or cutting out in paper several sets of separate bodies, heads, tails and legs—move these around and mix them up and the successful birds will be seen as against the dull ones. Now find out why some birds look lively others dead or static.

This exercise can be applied to animals too, the sizes and positions of heads, emphasis of body structures and placing of legs in relation to these gives quite different characters to them according to disposition but it must be repeated that decorations based on birds or animals can only be successfully attempted if the sources of ideas are sufficiently well understood.

The patterns and surface textures found on all these creatures are an inspiration in themselves for embroidery, fur, feathers, fins and scales and their decorative qualities, all vary according to the light falling on them. They are bold or subdued, clear cut or blurred and many of them suggest methods in which they could be worked as they look like embroidery beforehand. For careful observation of these, stuffed birds and animals are useful. Visit a natural history museum rather than a zoo, without drawing the complete creatures, as their patterns are a source of design. Reptiles and insects and various sea creatures can be studied from this aspect too in a museum and the patterns will be found very useful for filling areas in designs based on quite different subjects and for such purposes as dress and interior decoration.

Profiles give more scope for design than front or three-quarter views in which perspective adds difficulties. Details of parts of animals and birds are as interesting as complete ones when looking for ideas, and may be exaggerated or omitted in design, such as altering proportions or making patterns smaller or bigger or more regular. Decide which lines give the main movements, experiment by varying main proportions but start with simple positions, gradually changing them to more complicated ones. Pattern within shapes should emphasize movement and form, and is not suitable, placed at random and broken up into meaningless patches without regard for the contours as in reality pattern helps form even when used as camouflage.

Decide when designing from any of the forms in this section whether they are mainly angular or curved. Reduce them for simplicity to geometric shapes, then build them up again, increasing these characteristics to obtain more feeling of strength in the final designs.

Embroidery on woollen and cotton printed Swiss fabrics, approximately 84cm × 69 cm, using cretan stitch and couching, with herringbone on the striped cotton
Constance Howard

A hedgehog worked in various metal threads and padded gold kid
Jane Page

Exercise Cut single animals or birds in paper, combine them to make designs, cut several of the same species and repeat them as borders or all-over patterns, turn them round and rearrange. Cut more animals and birds, tearing off their heads, legs and tails. Give them different movements by re-arranging the separate parts. Turn the animal or bird shapes upside down or sideways and re-arrange them, combined or using either all animals or all birds. Use some of these shapes with plant form or geometric structures. From these exercises it is easy to develop abstract forms if wished, with all reality removed.

Other ideas will occur from these first experiments and quite complicated designs can result, although this will take patience and time.

170 *Three birds on a canvas sampler. Each is worked in a variety of stitches against a background of tent stitch. The sampler was worked to incorporate various stitches*
Kaye Norris

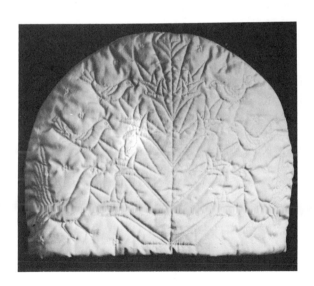

169 *A quilted tea cosy, 'Birds in a tree'. The reverse side shows a motif of birds in a nest* Kaye Norris

171 *A bird from pottery*

Victoria and Albert Museum

172 *Drawings of birds, emphasizing the sinuosity of their shapes*

173 *Patterns of geese. Wall paintings from the tomb of Neba-man, Thebes*   *British Museum*

174 Various birds, simplified from reality into semi-geo-
metric shapes

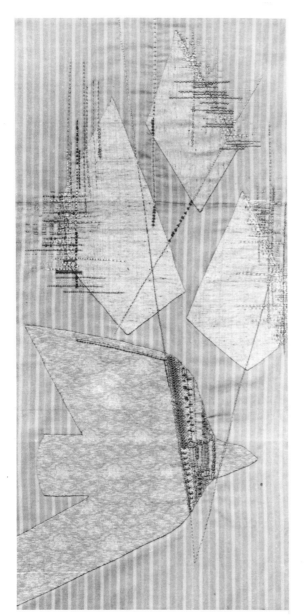

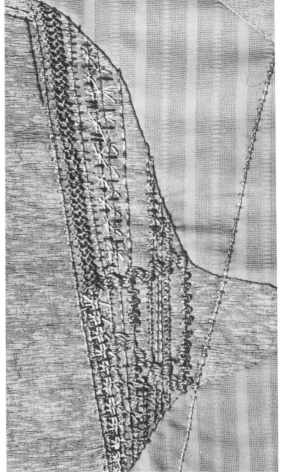

175 A pulpit fall showing a dove. A simple but pleasing symbolic shape is used here, avoiding unnecessary details
Anne Butler
A detail from the pulpit fall, with rich textures in stitchery. Creams and greys are the main colours

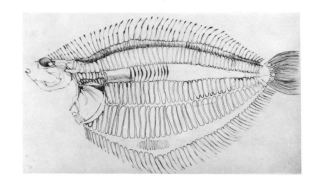

176 *Drawing of a fish skeleton*
  Hand embroidery freely worked, the tail is disjointed and
  does not balance the main idea
  Cut work, machine embroidery
  Idea based on some of the bones, machine embroidery

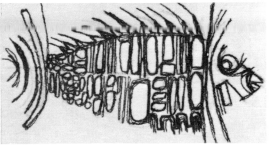

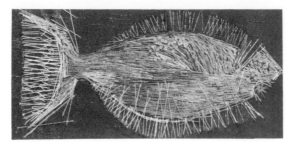
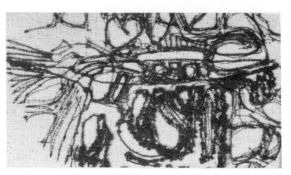

Above: hand embroidery
Right: machine embroidery based on joint structure. All the samples are based on the drawing of the skeleton
Brenda Holmes

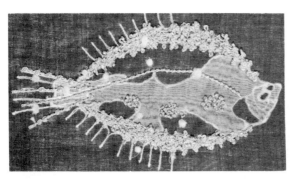

177 *A fish applied in organdie on to organdie. Machine embroidery*   *Josephine Canty*

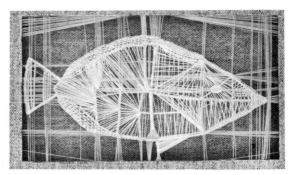

179 *A fish constructed on a network with weaving and stitchery combined*   *Mary Stanley*
Avery Hill College of Education

178 *Panel 'Fish', based on skeletal drawings. Appliqué and hand stitchery, in various materials*   *Marjorie Priestly*

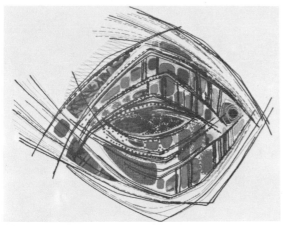

180 *Fish panel—a mosaic effect in various velvets and felts. Beads, machine and hand embroidery are incorporated*
Constance Howard

181 (a) *A fossil fish embroidered entirely in gold threads, kid strips and silks on green wild silk*
Pauline Watson

(b) *Detail of the fossil. French knots and small spots are embroidered in greenish brown filoselle. The whole embroidery is very richly textured and padded giving a feeling of depth*
Pauline Watson

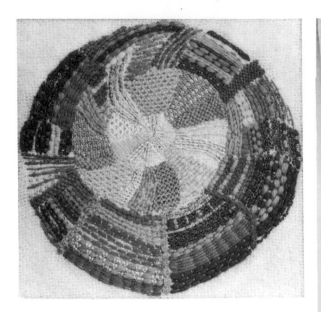

182 *A motif based on sea urchins*   Isobel Chapman

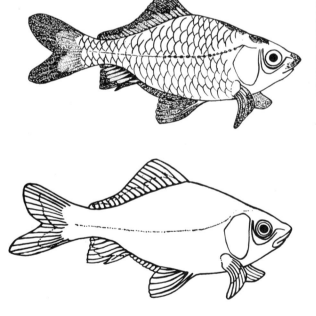

184 *A hanging 8 feet high, incorporating cats and lions in a heraldic manner. The animals are applied and covered with coarse stitchery, in rug wools and other thick threads. Main colours, reds, greys and yellows*   Jane Page

183 *A drawing of a golden carp*
   The carp without scales. The beginning of simplification, from reality to flat pattern

185 *Decorative fishes, based on the drawing of the carp*

186 A cat
   Cats, simplified for design
   Horses from Greek pottery in the Louvre
   Primitive animal on a pot in the Louvre

188 Kaleidoscope of small brilliant felt shapes giving a vital
piece of embroidery

Opposite *A porcupine on silk, embroidered in various gold
threads* Barbara Dawson

189 Bison, on wool worked in wools with heavy textures.
   The animal is almost geometric in form but in spite
   of the rigidity of its shape has a semblance of strength
   Ioné Dorrington
   Detail showing the coarse stitchery

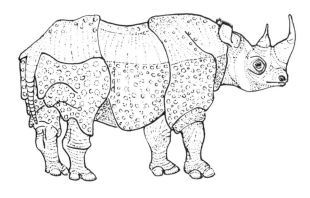

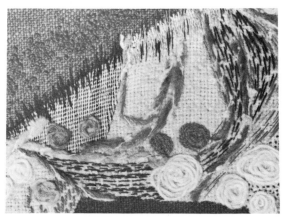

187 Pattern on a rhinoceros which increases the feeling of
form and gives solidity to it

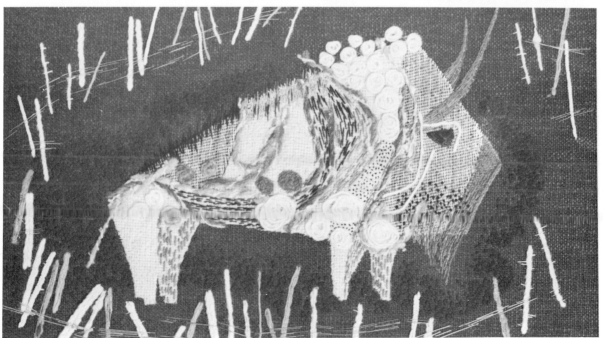

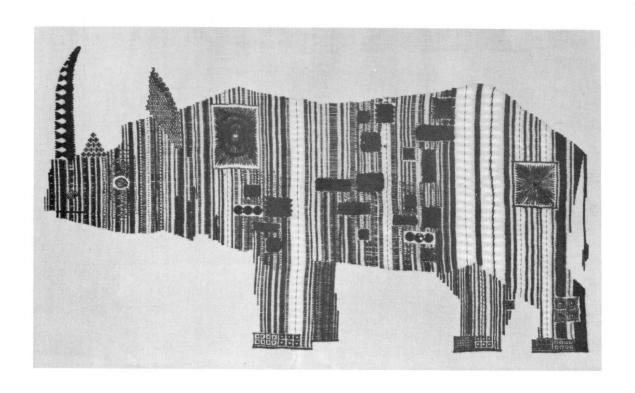

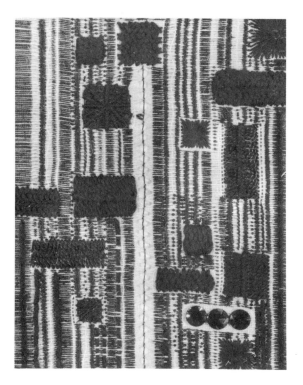

190 (a) *A rhinoceros on hessian in drawn and pulled stitchery, darning and jet beads. This embroidery gives the heavy clumsy feeling of the animal, obtained by the closer stitchery of the head which becomes darker in contrast to the more open stitchery of the body*   Doreen Elliott

(b) *Detail of part of the body. Many of the patterns worked on the animal are suitable for dress embroidery*

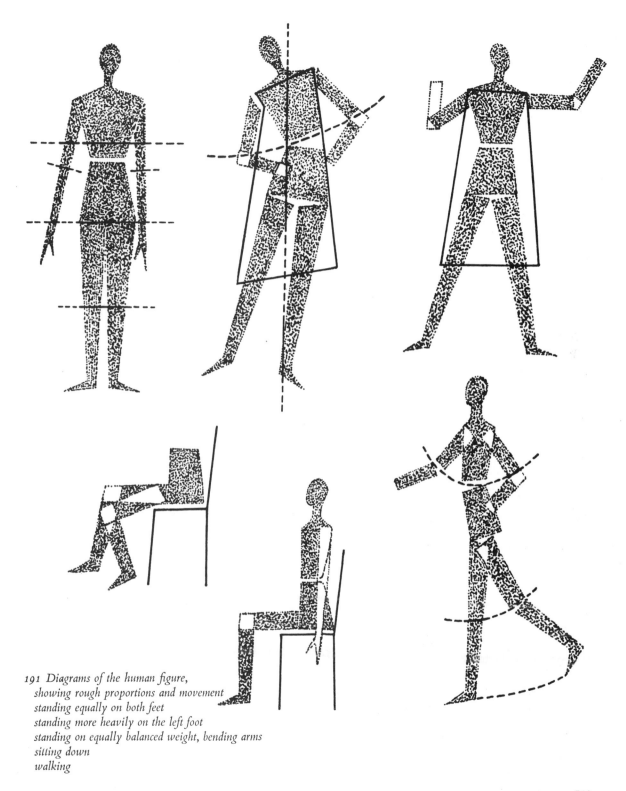

191 Diagrams of the human figure,
showing rough proportions and movement
standing equally on both feet
standing more heavily on the left foot
standing on equally balanced weight, bending arms
sitting down
walking

The human figure is the most difficult to study but also the most interesting as a source of design, as it has been throughout the ages. Today it is less used for embroidery as it is difficult to eliminate all illustrative quality from the designs and with pure abstraction it loses much of its meaning as the figure tends to disappear.

It is again, quite impossible to base designs upon figures without understanding their structures. As in watching birds and animals a start must be made by looking at people moving about their everyday occupations. Watch people walking or running, how do they move, what do their arms and legs do? What happens when they sit down? Which way to their joints bend—knees, elbows, wrists and ankles? What is the difference in proportion between an adult and a child? All these questions can only be answered by constant observation, then sketching and making notes which solve the problems, and by watching all kinds of people in various positions and occupations, such as sitting, standing, running, bending, stretching, ad infinitum. This observation should help in understanding the general proportions of the figure, the position of the waist, hips, and knees in relation to the whole, the placing of the elbows and hands in relation to the waist and knees, the size of head in proportion to the whole. All these vary according to the individual height but a good general average in designing is sufficient. The hip-line roughly divides the figure in half horizontally, the elbows often dig into the waist, the hands hang half way between hips and knees, the head is proportionately larger in a child than in an adult, the younger the child the larger this appears; the adult figure is often more curved or more angular than that of a child, which appears straighter.

Look in a mirror to remember these rough proportions then try to imagine the figure as a series of rectangles or cylinders. Cut out in paper a simple standing figure based on rectangles. This may be done symmetrically by folding the paper vertically, cutting one-half vertically from head to foot. Tear the arms and legs at the joints, tear the body at the neck and waist and re-assemble to give an appearance of movement. The problem of balance will occur here, for if the figure is standing on both feet, the balance will be equal, but immediately this alters and the figure leans or stands more heavily on one foot than the other, changes instantly occur. Practise standing in different positions before a full length mirror and see what happens. The shoulders and hips sway towards each other on one side, away from each other on the other side of the body, the spine curves and the feet are unequally placed on the ground. If a plumbline is held at the pit of the neck and allowed to fall to the ground it will be found that the firmly planted foot is immediately below the pit of the neck in a straight line, taken from the front view of the figure. In a profile view in which movement is transient the plumb-line falls through the supporting foot as the weight is transferred over it. Study movement until simple smooth shapes can be cut out rather as geometric figures than real ones. Make some of these curved, some angular, change the positions of heads and arms but keep the balance of the legs. All details should be ignored at this stage but particular characteristics may be emphasized, such as very tall figures with small heads, wide thick set figures, triangular or square figures or cylindrical ones. Eliminate true perspective, and parts of the figures not required in the design, sometimes arms are unnecessary, sometimes feet. Clothe the figures after the basic movements have been worked out, again keeping to very simple shapes. Two colours of paper are useful for this, one for the figures, another to lay over

192 Diagrams of the human figure. Whenever possible, study should be made from a live model
   unclothed, clothed and elongated
   reduced to simple geometric shapes—triangles, and balanced
    on one foot more heavily than on the other
   child and adult proportions
   child and adult—from a sculpture
   geometric treatment of the figure
   heads from various sources

them with costume, which again is affected by movement, as is seen in the drapery on mediaeval ecclesiastical embroidery, or in a seated clothed figure compared to a standing one.

Heads, hands and feet require detailed study before they can be reduced to simplicity but if the head is imagined as a cube or egg shape, the hands and feet as a series of wedges this is a beginning. The features, fingers and toes are difficult to draw but by looking in a mirror for a sufficient time before drawing, it will be easier; then drawing from memory will give an indication of how much is known, how much forgotten about both details and complete figures. In design it is important to understand the figure sufficiently to forget its reality.

The head has always proved of interest to the designer, it has qualities which make it exciting as a subject for design. First of all look at as many different heads as possible and find out why they are dissimilar. Although every head has the same number of features their placing within the framework of the face is different, as is the shape of the face. The ones most important for character should be enlarged, such as the eyes or mouth. The hairline grows differently and the placing of the head on the neck is very important in obtaining character. Try to reduce the features to simple geometric shapes, cut them in paper and place similar ones within different frameworks, then cut a variety of differently proportioned features and try them out within the same framework. Note the effects and choose one successful one and one less successful. Analyse these two designs trying to find out why one works the other does not. It may be difficult at first but it is only by doing this that appreciation is built up. Differently shaped heads and hair styles can be tried too—the variety is infinite. Some are very long, some square, some oval, these shapes should be exaggerated with features to correspond.

If further inspiration is required look at figures and heads produced by other peoples, study archaic and mediaeval sculpture and ceramics or primitive painting, icon painting, native interpretations such as masks and ritual figures; then look at works produced by artists such as Manzu,

Morini, Henry Moore, Modigliani, Picasso who are particularly interested in the human figure and the head. In embroidery the simpler the interpretation the better but neither a painting, sculpture nor illustration is the answer, but a two-dimensional shape which expresses a figure without too much detail. This is still one of the most difficult but one of the most fascinating things to accomplish and a problem still to solve completely successfully.

193 Head, embroidered by a six-year-old girl

195 *A head, with features worked on net and darned to give an effect of contour. A panel on blue wild silk, embroidered by hand and machine*   Janet Graham

194 *A head based on one embroidered in coloured threads on a Cretan petticoat flounce in the Victoria and Albert Museum. This head is worked entirely in metal braids and gold kid appliqué, with fine couched thread round the ear-rings. The features are geometric in treatment and the result symmetrical*

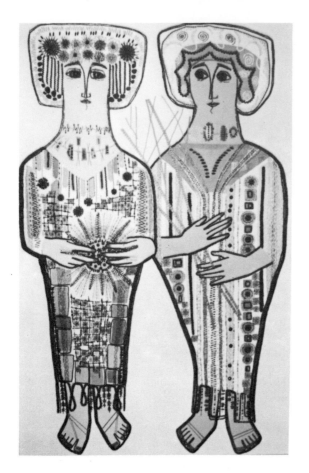

196 (a) Two figures—illustrative in treatment, based on
Etruscan pottery. The emphasis of head size gives added
weight to that of the figures   Constance Howard
   (b) Detail of the heads of the Etruscan figures which are
more allied to line drawings than stitchery, but are in keeping
with the style of feet and hands

197 Four angels. A panel for a children's chapel embroidered on striped Finnish cotton. Small applied shapes, embroidery in heavy threads, metal couching and laid work make up the bodies of the figures. The features are couched solidly, the wings are worked in heavy threads, in Portuguese border and raised chain-band stitches together with other stitches

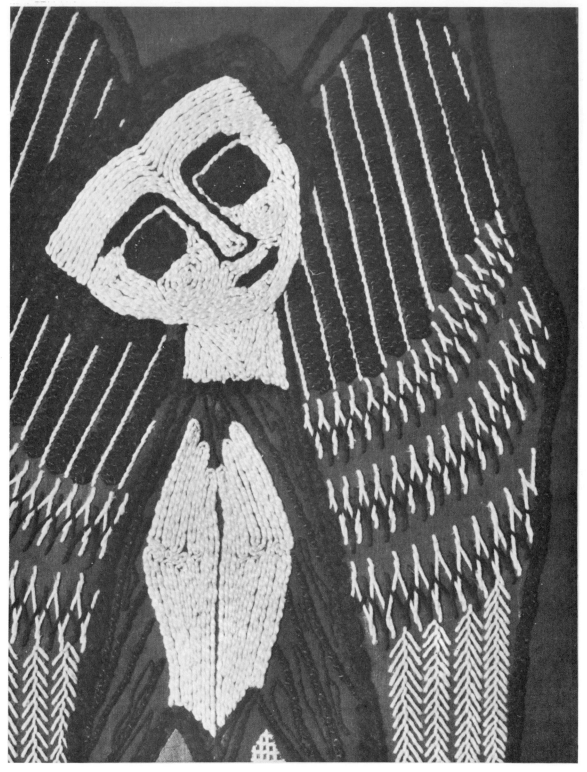

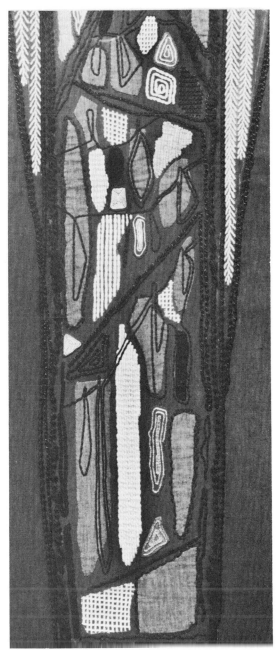

Detail showing couching of head and hands in perlita, to give an effect of contours

Detail of part of the body of an angel, appliqué and laid work

Another detail Constance Howard

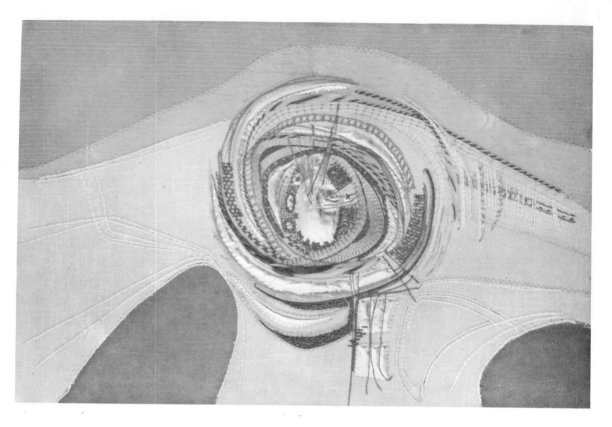

*198 An abstract panel 'Nebulae'. Appliqué with padding.
Metal threads and various materials   Janet Graham*

Man-made products are mostly static and are therefore more easily studied at leisure. Practically everything can be used as a basis of design for embroidery, from architecture to small tools and implements, screws, tangled wire, household implements and anything which creates inspiration.

Study the main overall shapes first of all, the detail afterwards. Look at things from all possible angles to decide from which the most interesting design could be made. See the shapes first of all as silhouettes which eliminate perspective. Take parts of objects and enlarge or reduce them as necessary. Leave out parts which do not help the design and emphasize those which give character. Move shapes around, turn them upside down and sideways, try out positive and negative patterns by changing the tone emphasis. Add detail as required but only after the main basic shapes have been planned satisfactorily.

By working out all design, step by step and by making sure that number one is as good as possible before commencing on number two, a satisfactory result should be achieved in the final design. Whatever reality has been the inspiration behind the idea, when it is thoroughly understood, proportions may be modified, exaggerated and altered, details omitted or added and generally all rules broken. The essential point is that the design can be embroidered and will not be an imitation of painting or illustration but will use to the full the exciting qualities particularly applicable to the craft.

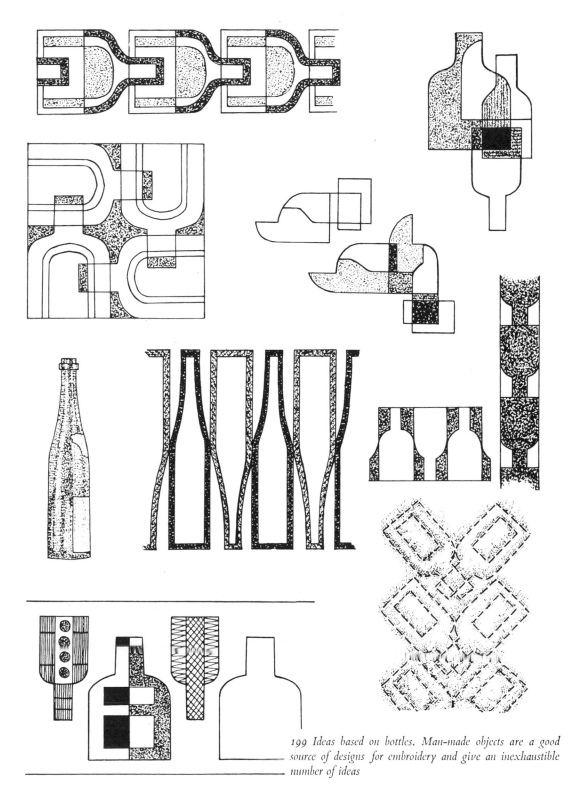

199 Ideas based on bottles. Man-made objects are a good source of designs for embroidery and give an inexhaustible number of ideas

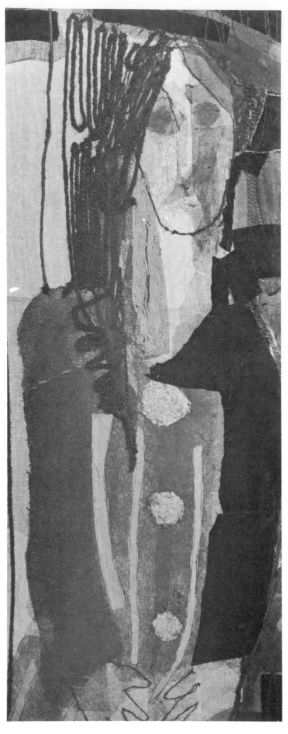

Abstract design Today there is a preponderance of abstract painting and design. It is an important part of art but must not preclude all other forms. It is non-representational as compared with obviously derivative design but it contains other important elements of form.

The dictionary definition of abstract is—separated from, existing or thought of existing apart from material objects—as opposed to concrete. It is ideal not practical. To abstract is to remove, take away by mental or physical operation.

There are two ways in which abstract ideas may be developed:

1 Is to start with the study of natural or manmade forms, ignoring the surface qualities and to select those forms or shapes which retain the inherent character of the objects studied, but are reduced to the non-representational; or by selection of parts of objects from which designs based on their surface textures or superficial qualities are made, such as designing from tree bark or pebble veining, resulting again in pure, non-representational shapes.
2 To start with the shapes, themselves abstract, such as geometric ones, or forms accidentally arrived at, or selected arbitrarily from the surrounding background.

In either case the basic rules for design apply, proportion and placing of shapes, colour and tone, in fact they are of greater importance as in designs of this type where there is no illustrative quality, the tensions between shapes and colours are of main interest, the direction of line and shape, the impact of pure complementary colour as contrasted with that of lesser strength, must be felt on looking at the work which has no recognizable context.

Embroidery possesses all the attributes for successful abstract pattern and is one of the best mediums in which to work out these ideas but this form of design is not easily accomplished and it is more profitable if some of the simpler approaches are practised and understood before attempting this field of work, hence the reason for this section being placed at the end of the chapter, rather than at the beginning.

200 Panel with a figure. Here applied nets give tone and a subtle effect of depth   *Patricia Brenner*

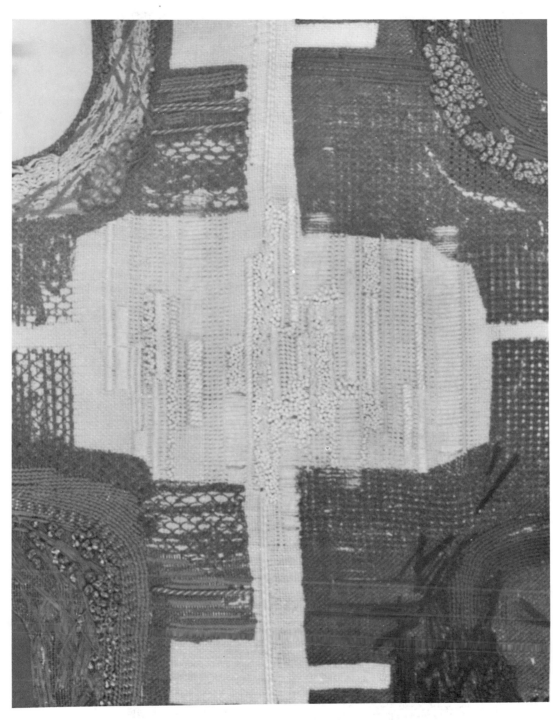

201 *Abstract panel. The background is printed, the textures richly worked within the printed pattern*
Heals IP' *Cynthia Sharpe*

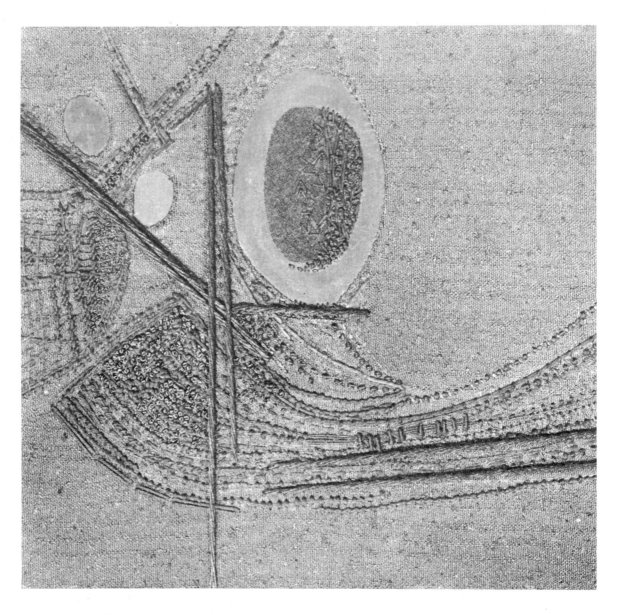

*202 Abstract panel, 'Inlaid shapes' in a variety of black
materials   Anne Butler*

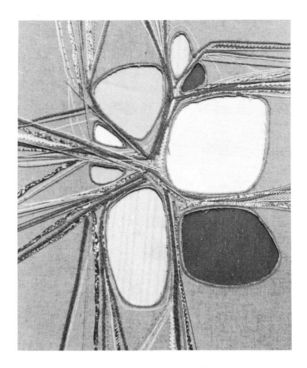

203 *Abstract panel with shapes recessed behind holes cut in the upper layer of fabric 'Sun IV'* Rosalind Floyd

204 *Knotted cable chain stitch worked in perlita, soft anchor and perle, for a border on a child's skirt. All white threads* Pauline Watson

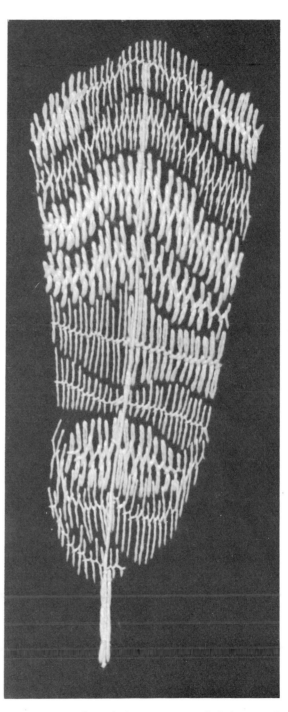

205 *Cretan stitch worked in a variety of thicknesses of thread—a feather. The difference in appearance of the stitches depends on the thickness of thread used and the amount of fabric taken up by the needle* Barbara Conroy

Texture, Colour, Tone

Texture is a quality of surface which can be felt by touching; everything has its particular texture by which it may be recognized blindfold. It is an integral part of embroidery in which the variations in surface quality are limitless within its particular field. In hand embroidery the finest lace-like quality to that of heavily padded and raised stitchery give much variation of surface; in machine embroidery fine effects with contrasting knobbly textures are possible but there is less contrast than in hand stitchery as both threads and techniques are limited to a narrower range. The rich textures which may be found in embroidery are not imitable in other mediums, therefore they should be exploited to the full in this craft.

Texture should not be confused with surface pattern although each may be used in breaking up a plain area. A pattern may be painted on paper consisting of a number of similar units repeated at definite intervals but these cannot be felt although a semblance of texture can be represented in the paint. The same pattern could be translated into embroidery with raised stitchery and would then contain both texture and pattern. A haphazard cluster of french knots to fill a given area constitutes a texture but not a pattern but an arrangement of french knots spaced at definite

and regular intervals over the same surface would make a pattern although the knots still give a texture. Bark on a tree trunk can be felt, it is often rough and lumpy, this character may be represented in stitchery by threads of various kinds, the effect is still rough on the fabric, and gives an irregular effect not consistent with a pattern although it has texture, but if a painting of the bark is made on paper in water colour there is no real texture but only a symbol of it unless paste is mixed with the colour to raise it from the flatness of paint, or it is done in thick oil-colour.

The materials used in embroidery already have textures, perhaps delicate or coarse, shiny or dull. The technique may be one in which the background is covered with stitchery, drawn up into holes, cut, or darned in patches, padded, or covered with small stitches to vary the surface in parts. Without contrast of texture embroidery is boring and lacks vitality although too much variety in texture and too many different stitches used together with many colours gives complete confusion. Monochrome embroidery such as net work, pulled work and drawn thread work rely more on texture than colour for effect, in fact are less successful if contrasting coloured threads are used for the stitchery, as the essence of these techniques is their open and often lace like quality which would look cluttered if worked in many colours.

The choice of both fabrics and threads for embroidery is important, the range of textures being very wide, therefore they should be chosen with the purpose and technique in mind. The background may be firm and smooth as in fine linen, lawn or worsted, silky as in taffeta, wild silk or organza, knobbly as in some woollens, coarse linens and some furnishing fabrics. The cloth may be fine like gauze, heavy as in rep or hessian, or very loosely woven as in scrim or some of the Swedish curtain fabrics, it may be rich as in brocade, velvet or satin, even woven with metal threads or lurex. The list is endless as all the natural fibres are imitable in 'man-made' ones which are much wider in range than the non-synthetic. According to the purpose of the embroidery, the choice of fabric and subsequent technique will be determined. Textures particular to one method of work may be combined with others such as open-work and padded satin stitch, seen in Ayrshire and Hedebo work, or quilting and surface stitchery, popular during the eighteenth century.

Threads alone are interesting, thick, coarse and dull such as rug wools, shiny cords, thinner ones like anchor soft cottons, No. 6 linen threads, No. 3 to 8 sylko perle, down to stranded cottons, various wools, from soft embroidery and tapestry to finely twisted crewel ones, raffias, metal and lurex threads, strings, weaving threads of all kinds to the finest of machine cottons, all have their uses. One stitch worked in each of these different threads would look completely dissimilar and a worthwhile and interesting basis for a series of exercises.

Anything may be used in embroidery to create interesting textures, providing that the materials chosen are workable. Beads, sequins, buttons, mirror glass, glass, leather and kid, metal, shells and small stones, seeds, bark and wood shavings are all possibilities employed in the right context. An imaginative use of unusual materials is a point to stress in designing for the craft, as long as the result is not gimmicky and at the expense of taste and sensibility or experiment for the sake of being different.

Embroidery can be sumptuous worked entirely in one colour or in one contrasting coloured thread throughout as the texture treated by variability of type of thread and stitchery will give depth. In appliqué similarity of colour but contrast in texture, such as black velvet applied to black wool or black organdie, cream satin on cream wool or a dull fabric, natural suede or leather on natural hessian are exciting even without the addition of threads and stitchery but with self-coloured or many-coloured embroidery very rich effects are possible.

A means of obtaining textures is to change the character of the original fabric by embroidering into it rather than in working on its surface (see figs 9 and 10). Darning on linen or net, tying threads together, removing some and inserting others, looping or knotting working threads into the spaces made by tying or extracting, tufting or covering the fabric entirely with stitchery such as in canvas embroidery or in some cross stitch, all help to enrich and vary the original surface.

Blind appliqué, or patchwork, with contrasting textures is successful without stitchery, providing that the design is well spaced and envisaged as mass rather than line. To obtain contrast of surface flat smooth stitches may be combined with knotted or chunky ones, such as satin stitch and double knot, raised chain band and long and short stitch, laid work with interlaced stitches. Coarse threads worked on fine fabrics such as thick soft cotton on muslin, plastic raffia on net, for the decoration of summer clothes or household articles, are successful providing that the stitchery is carefully chosen to suit those threads. Fine machine stitchery combines well with heavy hand embroidery, shapes filled by textures made with a massing of french knots, seeding, beads and sequins are exciting used in contrast with smooth areas of stitchery such as laid work or close couching, or with areas of undecorated fabric.

Machine embroidery has textural possibilities different from those of plain stitching and quite coarse results are obtained by experiment and with experience. By winding a thicker thread such as anchor soft cotton or sylko perle on the bobbin, with a fine machine cotton on the top tension, lines of cable stitch looking like beading can be worked on the side of the fabric facing downwards on the machine. The stitch length should be adjusted to give the effect needed. An even more interesting texture is obtained by free stitching with the pressure foot removed, the feed dog dropped and the under tension loosened to its utmost and although this method does not work on all machines it is worth trying out. The fabric to be embroidered is stretched in a ring frame with the right side of the embroidery facing the bed of the machine, the upper tension is tightened to its utmost and by working freely the thick thread in the spool is looped, giving an appearance of turkish towelling or chenille; lines and solid textures may be worked in this way and combined with delicate openwork patterns, also worked on the machine, strong textural contrasts are obtained. A coarse thread such as number 30 machine cotton, worked on a fine fabric like organdie is effective, and with a zigzag attachment to the machine a great number of results are possible, all giving varied textures. Machine embroidery on net or embroidery by hand may be fine or coarse, open or closely worked, or a combination of the two methods. It is effective texturally either way if following a well planned design.

All the varieties of textures mentioned, and many more are part of the fascination of the craft, the combinations and permutations of fabric, thread and stitch are endless. This means that no two pieces of embroidery are exactly alike although starting from a common source of inspiration, even the working of the same stitch in similar thread by two individuals gives a different result.

Colour is one of the most personal means of expression and gives individuality to work. Colour can have a serious effect on outlook causing irritation, excitement, calmness or depression and plays an important part in surroundings. On looking at objects it is often the colour which first attracts attention and it is well known that children and primitive races see colour before they are aware of form. Colour is a medium entirely relative to its environment and is never what it appears to be as it is affected by light, texture, adjacent colours and other variable considerations.

Everyone sees colour differently and one stabilized colour will appear diversely to two people, although seen under the same conditions and almost from the same angle and lighting. Each has an individual and favourite colour scheme and tends to ignore others which do not conform to this preference, as those schemes disliked are usually due to previous associations and a lack of understanding of what can be achieved with colour. It is impossible to work with a colour which is hated but if the knowledge in combining colours is widened, these prejudices can be broken down. If non-typical colour schemes are tried out occasionally the interest in the use of colour increases, the preconceived idea that 'red, pink and orange don't go' will gradually fade until it is realized that any colour will 'go' with any colour, providing that a few rules are understood.

With the right tones (see page 163), proportions and surfaces of colour any schemes work, there is no final theory of colour and the whole subject must be treated experimentally, guided by personal taste and feeling if it is to mean anything individually.

Perception of colour increases through observation and a good way in which to learn to appreciate the excitement in its discovery is to study natural form and environment (see pages 38, 96). To try to analyse the ranges of colour such as might be found in a shell or a flower head, a tree trunk or a brick wall, will both increase general interest and give a more subtle outlook on schemes of colour, and a list of colours can be written down (see page 14), trying to give them exact definitions, such as a pinkish brown or a bluish red, then spots of colour found to represent them; these may be fabrics, threads, paper, or if wished paint or crayon which is mixed as closely as possible to the description. It is even better if the source of the colour and the description are seen together to see if the description tallies with the reality and the matching of the colours corresponds to both. This exercise is difficult but leads to more acute and accurate observation and a better understanding of the changes which take place according to light, texture and juxtaposition with other colours. It will soon be seen that 'red' means little, is it a bright red, how bright? Perhaps it looks dark as it is surrounded by a paler colour, perhaps it looks warm and orangish or it may be a bluish red. When the matching colour has been made or found in a fabric, place this spot of colour against a completely different one from its original association. It will not look the same but darker or paler, warmer or colder, which leads to the conclusion that all colours have infinite variations. It is worthwhile spending time on matching or choosing colours for embroidery, as one wrong colour may ruin a complete piece of work, the right choice may change an ordinary work into something alive and interesting.

In studying nature it will be found that many colour schemes are within a narrow range and consist of variations of one or two colours related to each other, such as is found in some shells, foliage or stones, while others contain violent contrasts such as seen in some flower heads, butterfly wings and ripe fruit on trees against the leafy backgrounds. Broken surfaces, shiny surfaces and smooth ones tend to modify colour, for example if each were painted with exactly the same dye the results would look different. Therefore in choosing fabrics, threads and stitchery, each surface must be considered in relationship to the others, three reds of equal intensity but in different textures could be used together and look different as the reflection of light on the surfaces would appear to vary the depths of colours.

It is not necessary to go into great detail and theory of colour perception as long as the basic principles of colour usage are understood. Very simply there are the three primary colours, red, blue and yellow, the secondary colours, purple, green and orange, each a mixture of two of the primaries and the three tertiaries which are russet, olive and citron and are mixtures of the secondaries. In their strongest and purest forms the primary

colours are called hues. The pure hue mixed with black equals a tone or darker colour, the same hue mixed with white equals a tint or a paler colour, so that every colour can be varied either by the addition of another colour or by the addition of black or white to an infinite number of colours. The pure hue plus black and white equals grey, or black plus white equals grey. The former greys are called chromatic and may be varied towards reddish or perhaps bluish greys according to the colour mixed with them, the latter are called achromatic and can be varied only in darkness or lightness.

Tones In any colour scheme, tone is important and cannot be avoided (see page 163) but if embroidery has a drab, even appearance, some strongly contrasting tone introduced, either a lighter or darker one, can liven it up considerably. Colours are affected by those surrounding them and to say that one is brighter or lighter than another is relative. The same colour against a darker background looks brighter than it does against one lighter in tone than itself. This may be proved by using coloured papers or fabrics and experimenting with them. The colours will appear different together yet remain constant on their own. Some will appear to change considerably, some very little. Proportion of one colour to another gives an apparent change in tone.

206 *Sampler using a variety of black materials to give a rich effect both in texture and tone* Goldsmiths

Exercise If two similar small spots of colour are placed on large differently coloured areas, each spot appears different both in depth and intensity. Try several different sets of colours in this way and try to find out how each changes such as an orange spot on red, and the same spot on neutral grey, or pale blue. Some spots of colour will be more affected than others. Try the same idea using threads and it will be found that the complication of texture and stitchery gives even more variations in colour. Some colours appear to jump out of the background, some recede, try them in stitchery and this appearance will become modified. Break up the prominent colour and work the receding one smoothly and closely and it will come forward if its background has remained constant in colour, while the other will recede. Working one coloured thread vertically with another colour across horizontally gives infinite variety. The size of an area may be modified by colour relationship, a plain blue on white looks larger than blue on black, find out why and experiment again with different depths of colour put together, using small areas on larger ones and large areas with narrow surrounds.

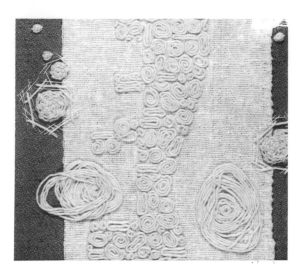

208 Detail of textures from a panel. Cream wool applied to scarlet wool, embroidered in hand-spun cream wools and stranded cotton, giving a rough appearance

Ioné Dorrington

207 Detail from 'Heal II' figure 201

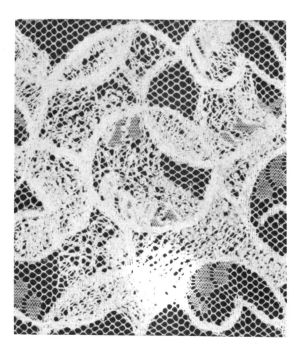

209 Machine embroidery on a lace background. This adds to the quality of the original fabric, as it enriches it

Goldsmiths

210 Freely worked machine satin stitch, giving a chunky texture   Molly Arnold

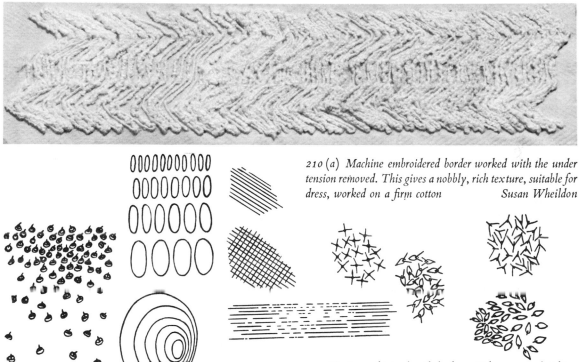

210 (a) Machine embroidered border worked with the under tension removed. This gives a nobbly, rich texture, suitable for dress, worked on a firm cotton   Susan Wheildon

211 Textures obtained with broken stitchery, cross hatching repetition of a stitch, variously spaced. Small units closely and more openly placed together

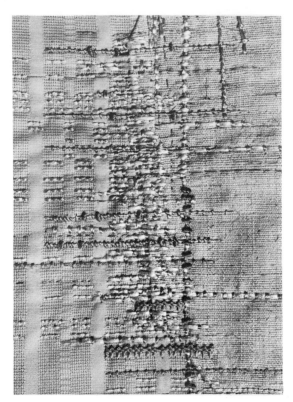

213 A detail of stitchery on a pulpit fall, mainly in couching and raised knots, giving a broken surface quality

Anne Butler

212 A caterpillar in which the exciting textures are the main interest. The idea evolved from the striped woollen background and the embroidery is worked in various threads, beads and sequins in dark greens, blacks and other near tones

Anna Wilson

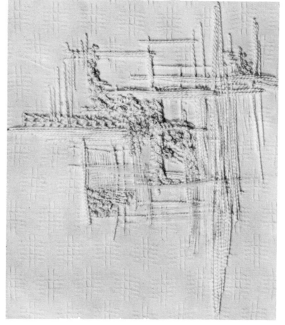

214 An all white sampler with contrast in the use of free-line stitchery and knotted and raised effects

Goldsmiths

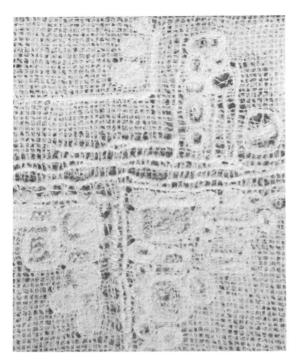

215 *An all white, machine embroidered sampler on a very loosely woven woollen*

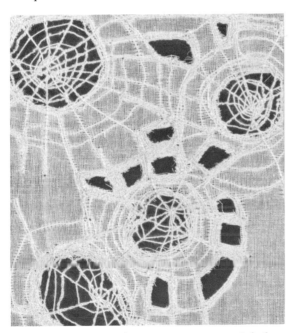

216 *Number 30 machine sewing cotton stitched on muslin, giving a strong contrast to the fabric. First attempt at free-cut work* Goldsmiths

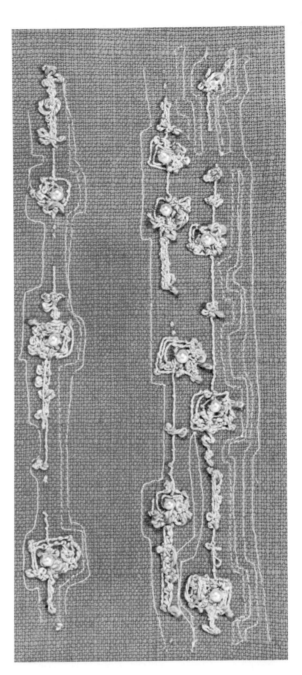

217 *Contrasting coloured and textured threads and pearls used together, with free machine stitching in a coarse machine cotton* Molly Arnold

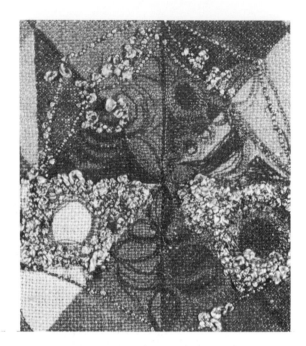

218 *A printed background of coarse linen-type fabric, embroidered in machine stitchery with machine cotton and perle* *Goldsmiths*

219 *A panel using various materials and a wide variety of threads* *Goldsmiths*

220 *Cane, string and embroidery threads combined in a semi-woven, semi-embroidered decoration. The textures are obtained with the crossing and looping of threads*
Joan Ingram
Avery Hill College of Education

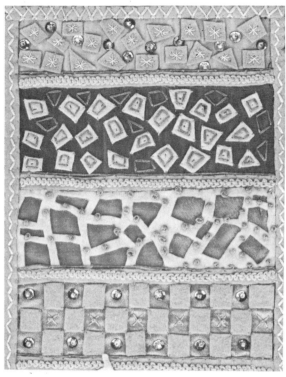

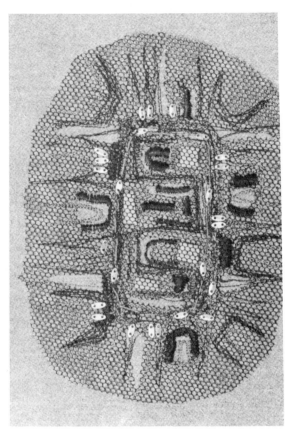

221 *Felts, satins and silks, beads and sequins combined to give a mosaic-like texture. The small cut-out felt shapes are used on the plain fabrics to give depth; in this way they are not wasted. Behind the holes of the cut shapes, silks and rich fabrics are placed, giving a 'paving' effect* Goldsmiths

222 *A combination of net on wool, small metal shapes and machine embroidery* Rosalind Floyd

223 *A combination of textures, drawn thread, with laid work, wooden buttons and eyelets* Josephine Windebank

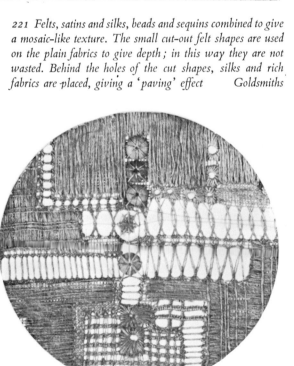

Exercise Use two simple shapes of a dark colour and place one of them on a dark background of similar tone, the other on a lighter background of similar area, note which shape appears darker.

225 *A motif for dress worked in spirals of stitchery which give an effect of light and shade by their direction. Light stitchery on a dark ground*

226 *A similar motif worked on a light background in dark threads*

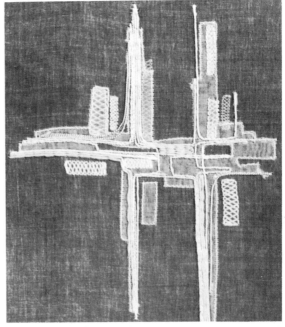

224 *Texture obtained from the basic material—Swedish curtain fabric; in which threads have been tied together pulled into holes and moved around. French knots and a variety of china and wooden beads have been incorporated in the design which shows part of a large flower*   Flora Walton

227 *All white embroidery, with organdie on fine wool, shadow work and couching*   Goldsmiths

228 *A motif in a variety of black textures which gives different tone values* Lynn Jones

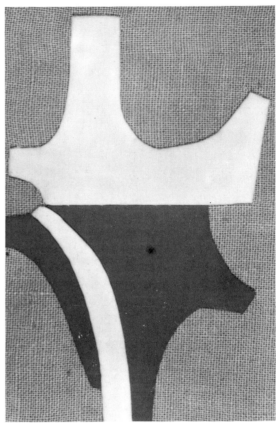

229 (a) *Blind appliqué using different fabrics together* Barbara Conroy

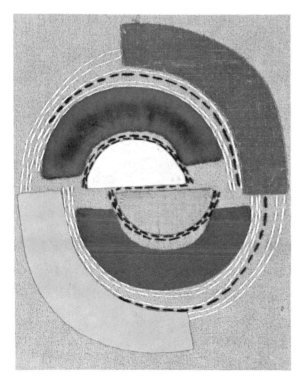

229 (b) *Blind appliqué* Constance Howard

230 Direction of stitch giving variations in tone. The drawings show darning and satin stitches

231 (a) Squares of differently toned fabrics used together—black, white and grey

(b) Felt shapes cut to show apparent changes in size by reversing tones

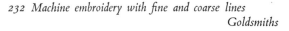

232 *Machine embroidery with fine and coarse lines*
Goldsmiths

233 *A panel in black, white and grey, with a printed background and with black organdie overlaid, producing the grey tones. Fine machine stitching and hand embroidery are combined. The design is based on the repetition of curves and squarish shapes, but the vitality is obtained by the strongly contrasting tones* Annwyn Morgan

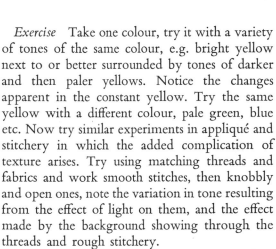

Exercise Take one colour, try it with a variety of tones of the same colour, e.g. bright yellow next to or better surrounded by tones of darker and then paler yellows. Notice the changes apparent in the constant yellow. Try the same yellow with a different colour, pale green, blue etc. Now try similar experiments in appliqué and stitchery in which the added complication of texture arises. Try using matching threads and fabrics and work smooth stitches, then knobbly and open ones, note the variation in tone resulting from the effect of light on them, and the effect made by the background showing through the threads and rough stitchery.

Colour is often said to be warm or cool in effect, those colours tending towards the reddish or orange hues being warmer, those tending towards bluish hues being cooler. A red with a bluish tendency may be cold compared with a red with an orange tendency, while a blue which is reddish is warmer than a blue which is more turquoise. A successful scheme of colour tends mainly towards one of these groups, equal amounts of warm and cold colours do not look well together as they fight with one another and neither dominates. Warm colours appear more prominent than cool ones, if a colour scheme of yellow ochre and turquoise were used, or one combining a reddish purple with a bluish purple, the ochre and the reddish purple would appear more dominant than the turquoise and bluish purple. This result could be modified by breaking up these colours in stitchery, how could the reverse effect be achieved in which the cool

colours dominate? If two contrasting tones of colour are used together such as a light fabric and a dark one of similar texture, the light one will appear brighter than it really is, while the dark one will appear deeper. This effect may be modified by surface stitchery in self-coloured threads which break up the fabric and give more tone with their shadows, if the embroidery is knobbly.

Warm colours appear warmer against cool, orange looks warmer against pale blue than with yellow ochre, similarly blue appears cooler against orange than next to blue green. Exercises to test out these effects may be tried with fabrics or coloured papers, using similar and dissimilar textures.

Proportions of colours in relation to one another in a scheme are very important. Equal amounts of each colour, of equal intensity are quite impossible to use, although, used in almost equal proportions, complementary colours can produce an effect of tension and vibration. The complementary colours are those which are opposite each other in the colour wheel and are roughly red opposite green; blue opposite orange; yellow opposite purple. A large area of one of these colours with a small area of the opposite or complementary one can be exciting and very exhilarating, such as a scheme mostly in reds, oranges and pinks with a small spot of bluish green or emerald; or a dark purple and blue scheme with small touches of yellow and orange. In schemes such as these the colours should be chosen from the same colour wheel, that is with colours of equal intensity, as there is an infinite number of wheels graduating from that with pure hues, through those mixed with black, becoming darker until black, and through those mixed with white which become paler until white.

Exercise Take three tones of any one-coloured paper, cut a number of rectangles of equal size in each and move them about getting different arrangements, the darkest at the top, then at the bottom and then in the middle, cut some rectangles less deep and put two of the unequal areas together to vary the proportions, see which arrangements look best, Why? It will be seen after experiment with the rectangles that unequal proportions of tone or colour look better than equal ones and that for balance, darker colours are better at the base, as in a striped fabric, the more interesting arrangement is of unequal widths of stripe rather than of equal ones. In other words one tone or colour should dominate, the others are subsidiary in the amounts used—the overall effect would be dark with touches of light or pale with darkish small areas or of one colour with tones obtained by the textures and directions of stitchery.

Exercise Using grey from the achromatic scale place it on differently coloured backgrounds and it will appear to change and take on a tinge of the complementary colour of this background, for example a medium grey on a bluish background will appear warmer and more reddish while on a creamish background it will appear cooler and more purplish in effect, although actually constant.

Large areas of colour tend to appear lighter than small spots of similar colour—this is important when buying background fabrics from looking at small samples. If complementary colours are used together and broken into small textures and spots they become insipid and merge, whereas two adjacent colours one on the other, such as red on orange or blue on green appear more vivid than if the colours were mixed, therefore in embroidery a greater brilliance of range is possible in using fabrics and threads rather than in using pigments. Patchwork could combine these theories very well.

It is important when embroidering an article to know if it is to be used in daylight or artificial light as the colours can be changed completely by different lighting, reds may become brown, yellows tend to disappear while blues and greens are intensified in depth. Again various textures will modify these effects, shiny ones being more effective as they reflect the light while opaque ones become duller, this is one of the reasons for glitter in embroidery on evening wear and a lack of woollen fabrics as they are dull surfaced and do not give such a lively appearance in artificial light, unless covered with beads and jewels or have glitter threads woven into them.

Many exercises may be invented to try out the theories of these suggestions, but by understanding them, as well as possessing a natural interest in colour and its complexities, unexpected and exciting results may be evolved. Delicate schemes, rich dark ones, brilliant ones, calm colour, vibrating or dazzling colour, all are possible and together with tone and texture the combinations are limitless and an unending source of experiment. Low toned schemes give greater subtlety than high toned ones and richer effects are obtained by using dark colours rather than pale ones but these again must be decided upon in relationship to the article being embroidered. The whole question of colour is an endless experiment, but a 'sense' of colour may be acquired by understanding some of the basic principles and then there is the fun of trying them out, eliminating those schemes which do not please, trying to analyse why they are unsuccessful and generally working with as wide a range of different colours as possible, so that choice is easier. The addition of tone and texture which is inseparable from embroidery adds to the difficulties of choice but necessitates this development of an awareness to colour.

Tone Having explained that tone is important in any scheme of work involving richness and apparent depth, it is necessary to understand its uses and particular values in embroidery as opposed to the use of pure colour.

Tone implies a variation between light and dark and is a means by which interest is given to a three-dimensional object or a flat decoration. The object will obtain this tonal quality by natural or artificial lighting which increases its air of solidity, the flat decoration by the application of colours varied in depth and intensity. The first impression of a piece of work is often of its colour which is then extended to a quality of darkness or lightness. In an embroidery the basic colour may remain stable, perhaps blue but it may vary in depth from navy to pale ice-blue. This is one use of tone in colour but in embroidery the textures of the materials, threads and stitchery can alter the tonal qualities, shiny surfaces reflecting light, opaque ones absorbing it, while raised stitchery

gives greater contrast in depth between light and dark than flat stitchery worked in one direction only.

In embroidery a great deal of variety of tone is obtainable without the use of colour, in fact some of the most exciting embroidery produced in the past has been in monochrome or self-coloured stitchery. Several methods may be used to give tonal richness to this work:

1 By direction of stitch: using a slightly shiny thread, an illusion of depth is obtained by working stitches in different directions so that light falls on these varied surfaces giving greater or lesser light and shade and apparent difference in colour. Satin stitch, split stitch, stem, chain, long and short, couching, fishbone and several others, working in blocks or spirally and at angles to one another create this tonal contrast. If colour as well as stitch direction is combined a wider range of tonal gradation is possible, laid work, damask darning and canvas work all having interesting possibilities.

2 By texture of stitch: again using self-coloured threads and placing small stitches such as french knots, bullion knots, seeding or running, very closely together, then more openly spaced so that more background is visible, an appearance of tone is created. Small beads are excellent for this kind of effect as their raised quality throws shadows on to the fabric.

3 By padding and raised stitchery which is again very much affected by the direction of light falling on it at an angle, whereby some parts of the embroidery are in shadow, others are highly lighted. Quilting is a good example of this, as stump work was in the seventeenth century and with closely worked parts as opposed to the larger, padded but unworked areas, strong contrasts of tone are possible.

4 By changing the nature of the fabric: pulling threads together into patterns leaving varying sized holes in between, which have a darker appearance than the material, such as in drawn fabric work, by removing threads

thus leaving large darker areas which can be re-woven with coloured or other threads as in needle weaving, or tied together as in drawn fabric work, the larger the holes the greater the tonal contrast. If the embroidery is on a dark background and lined with a light one, the reverse happens and holes are pale but give an opposite result tonally which is effective in a different way. Cut work would come into this category, together with eyelet holes.

5 By contrast of techniques, such as in Hardanger work where satin stitch is combined with cut holes and surface embroidery, eyelet or broderie anglaise combined with cut work and padded satin stitch, open lace fillings combined with heavy cotton embroidery on transparent or fine linen or muslin as in Hedebo work.

6 By combining shiny and dull materials, beads and sequins, metal threads, satin with wool, opaque fabric with transparent, tonal effects are achieved.

Other similar combinations of threads, stitchery and techniques can be thought of, in fact experiments along these lines could be very exciting, using self-coloured embroidery only.

Another method of obtaining good tonal contrasts is by using one colour of thread on a contrasting background, where the placing of the pattern is of first consideration, large areas being balanced by small ones, thin lines by thicker ones. Black work comes into this category, where the density of the pattern creates depth of tone from almost black, to paler tones with the more openly spaced ones; the contrast of smaller closer patterns with the open ones are the chief features of this kind of embroidery and to increase this contrast some patterns may be worked in two threads, some in one. They are all built up on the counted thread of the material.

Darning in a contrasting colour, with some close patterns and some open ones or some vertical and some horizontal, gives great variety of tone, or one colour using different weights of thread gives a similar effect. Darning on net in close and open patterns gives interesting tone and texture.

By working a design for one-colour embroidery so that some areas are closely stitched while others are more open, effects of tone are obtained, in fact this approach is worth exploring as it has many possibilities. Use black, grey and white paper for the spacing of the shapes into tones. It will be easier to translate into stitchery with similar tone values.

An interesting exercise in order to discover the relationship of form or space, to tone, is to take a design and work it in two different ways so that the tone values are reversed; where the tone values were dark in the first example, make them light in the second, try several small motifs in this way reversing the order of tone. The results will be quite different in each example.

It will be understood now that texture, colour and tone are highly integrated and, if thought out carefully, play an enormous part in the successful carrying out of a piece of embroidery. In fact without attention to each, a design cannot be wholly satisfactory when worked out.

Designing for Embroidery Based on Traditional Methods

In the past embroidery was often worked in styles introduced from foreign countries, was limited by materials, threads and colours available, or was worked in imitation of more costly articles such as lace, brocade and tapestry. Today there are few such limitations and the fact that black work was always carried out in black thread and quilting was worked usually in self-coloured stitchery should not now be a deterrent to a more varied and experimental outlook, with methods tried in reverse, such as with white stitchery on a black ground, quilting in coloured threads on contrasting backgrounds or drawn fabric worked with threads either darker or lighter than that of the fabric.

Unless the embroidery of the past is used as a basis for experiment there will be little progress in developing new ideas and methods of work, and it is only by considering different approaches that interesting results are achieved. Some of the traditional methods, after experiment with them, will still look better carried out as they were in the past, as there was often an aim in working them. In drawn fabric and drawn thread embroidery, for instance, its rich textures were evolved to give effects of lace-like surfaces rather than to show the working threads. Today with brightly coloured threads used on a contrasting background fabric, this lace-like quality of the past may be lost but the work gains a different character equally attractive, or conversely, by the intermingling of textures and colours may produce a muddled result.

Scale may be altered and normally fine work done on a coarse fabric with thick threads, such as translating drawn fabric on lawn to that done in raffia or string on hessian. As long as fabrics and threads are both changed proportionally, the result should be interesting, leading to more ideas in alteration of scale which may be exciting and quite different from what was expected.

Again, varied techniques may be combined on one piece of work. The choice of techniques must be considered in relation to one another, but several could be used together successfully on one article, in fact in the past there was not a rigid rule and some techniques were used with others very happily. If time is made in which to try out unusual combinations of styles, materials, threads and methods even if they are not always successful, eventually much better embroidery will be produced, and with a flavour of today instead of the past.

Experimental stitchery   Instead of working stitches in the accepted way, try them out differently by lengthening some and shortening others, by making them irregular rather than keeping them exactly the same, although this unevenness must be planned, as badly worked stitchery is not the same thing as deliberate irregularity. Stitches normally worked in rows may be detached, one length of thread need not necessarily be composed of the same stitch throughout, the width of the line being varied by change of stitch, with the embroidery turned around to make some of these and back again for others. Once the basic stitches of embroidery have been mastered, try them out first of all in a variety of threads as the results will be very different with each. Cretan stitch (page 147) has more variations in appearance than others as both the amount of fabric taken up by the needle and the angle at which it is placed in it, will give great difference in the result, and according to its method of working and the thickness of the thread used, it is suitable for different effects. Herringbone is another stitch which may be played with as it has so many uses, its character being altered in the same way as that of cretan stitch. Until the techniques in embroidery are understood thoroughly it is not possible to break away from them but once they are mastered it is time to find out what can be done to develop them further. The diagrams show some of the ways in which stitches may be varied. Experiment with each one and try to invent with it, make drawings of these inventions for future reference and in time a number of quite new stitches will evolve. If every embroideress did this it would be exciting to pool the ideas and would be a break through from the usual stitches seen in all embroidery books, most of which have been handed down from early times and have been copied with little change over the last four hundred years. One point must be remembered in working stitchery more freely, this is that the stitch must be suitable for its purpose and some of the very freely interpreted ones can only be used on wall decorations and similar embroideries, being too much on the surface of the fabric for hard wear. Some of the knotted stitches are a basis for more

invented ones, they are strong and suitable for articles which have to withstand wear and tear. Composite stitches, in which two or more are combined to make a third, may be seen in the diagrams and should give ideas for even further experiment. At any time the invention of new stitches will afford much interest and by using different thicknesses of thread, more variation in texture and surface quality is possible; in fact real experiment in embroidery is just beginning but as the craft is slow the findings of these will take time and the different approaches to embroidery which withstands hard wear and embroidery for wall decorations where surface appearance and excellence of design is of first importance, require versatility of mind and a very thorough knowledge of techniques in order to discard or use them at will.

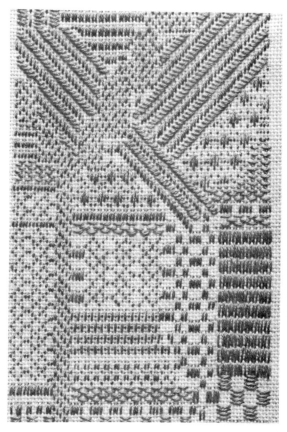

234 *A sampler containing a variety of darned patterns*
Barbara Conroy

Designing for particular types of embroidery

Each type of embroidery has its own characteristics and an understanding of these is invaluable in designing for different kinds of work. Some types hitherto done by hand are executed now, as well as and more speedily by machine, therefore it is a waste of time stitching them by hand except for the pleasure they may afford and the less mechanical effect achieved; broderie anglaise is an example of this; satin stitch, long and short stitch, petit point, chain stitch and smocking may be carried out successfully either by the domestic or by the trade machine but are less rigid when hand-worked and although exact repetition and perfection of technique was the sign of a first class embroiderer, today design is more important than mechanical exactitude which can be boring.

Machine Embroidery In designing for any machine embroidery the principle is the same, a continuity of stitching, so avoiding restarting the machine too often and wasting time. All machine embroidery is composed of lines of stitchery but if a zigzag attachment is built into the machine spots of satin stitch as wide as the swing of the zigzag are possible, or bands of satin stitch equal to the width of the swing of the zigzag may be worked. Much variety is obtained by using this zigzag freely and it is best to experiment with the machine to see what can be done before attempting any design. Lines of different weights, straight, curved or a combination of both, may be worked in ordinary machine stitching, by cable stitching on the underside of the fabric with a thicker thread in the spool, or by stitching down strings or rugwools with zigzagging or by ordinary stitchery if the threads are sufficiently soft. By placing a number of lines closely together a solid area is obtained, worked freely in different directions an all-over texture may be made and by using a thicker thread on the bobbin with the tension as loose as possible a raised loop stitch rather like Turkish towelling results, which gives a thick, solid effect.

Openwork and cut work shapes, whipped round the edges, with bars to connect the larger ones or with lace-like centres, may be designed as for cut work in hand embroidery, but if continuous repetitive pattern is required the shapes should be close together so that the throw over threads between each unit may be cut afterwards. Otherwise design for machine embroidery has many similar problems as for hand embroidery. (See specialist books on the subject.)

Hand Embroidery

Counted thread work The largest group in this section is of those embroideries worked on the counted thread of the material. There are several different kinds and in designing for them, squared paper is one of the most accurate methods of making the final drawings but it is non-spontaneous and gives a static result and it is unnecessary to use it unless very unsure of the technique being employed. Patterns may be worked by counting the threads as the work progresses, repetitive designs being quite easy to reproduce by this method. When these are non-repetitive and to fill whole areas, a chart of the design on squared paper is one method of planning as the whole idea may be more easily seen. In commencing a design for counted thread embroidery, rough sketches should first of all be made as in working out ideas for any type of stitchery, after which the final idea may be transferred to the squared paper, if this method seems more practical, and where each stitch may be indicated if necessary. The scale of the embroidery depends on its purpose and the fabric used; a coarse canvas such as that for making embroidered rugs would require large stitches in thick threads while a fine muslin with drawn fabric insets would give a lace-like quality in which the working thread is scarcely seen. Graph paper is available marked in squares of 6 mm to 2 mm and gives a sufficiently wide range for the purpose of most designs although it is possible to buy one more finely divided if necessary but remember that more freedom in working out is obtained with a less rigid approach to the design.

Assisi work is of Italian origin and based on cross stitch in which the background is worked leaving the pattern in the fabric with a double running outline round it and to indicate lines, within the shapes. As the pattern is mainly a silhouette and is traditionally worked with a blue or red background and a darker outline, it shows up as light against dark. In planning the rough idea, cut paper is the best method of obtaining simple shapes and in balancing the proportions of the patterns against those of the background. Rectangular and curved shapes are more easily worked in cross stitch than pointed ones and as it is the background which is embroidered this should be kept in mind.

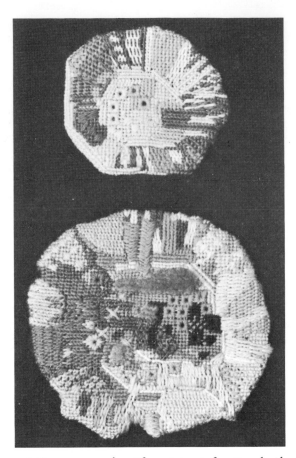

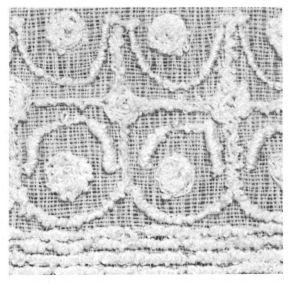

235 A border on scrim, machine stitchery with the under tension removed   Sally Thompson

236 Two canvas work motifs, reminiscent of coptic embroidery. Each is a combination of different stitches worked in silks and wools, giving rich textures   Diana Springall

237 Assisi embroidery, the background is in cross stitch, the details in double running stitch. The idea is based on buildings
Barbara Conroy

Blackwork is of Elizabethan origin, and was probably based on the earlier Spanish blackwork of Moorish descent. It consists of fine, lace-like patterns worked in black threads, one to two strands of stranded cotton, sewing syklo or silk or very fine tightly twisted wool, or any other thread, according to the coarseness of the background fabric; the patterns being built up in small back stitches or double running stitches over the counted threads of the fabric to make smaller or larger all-over ones. According to the closeness or openness of these patterns and whether one or two strands of stranded cotton are used the tonal variations and texture in the whole design are achieved. Metal threads may be used to advantage with some kinds of black work and were often introduced to add richness to traditional work. Simple shapes, not too small or the fillings will be difficult to work, should be planned to give both variety in area and in tone. Thick outlines or none at all are permissible and if double running is used entirely for the stitchery, both sides will be alike. (Pages 94 and 112.)

Canvas work In this embroidery the whole surface of the fabric is covered with stitchery, entirely in one type or with a number of different stitches, which give varied textures, some being hard wearing, some more for decoration, as they are looser and give longer threads on the surface. This type of work is one of the oldest known and may be done on linen or on any fabric in which the threads can be counted and, according to the choice of stitches, on a single or double thread canvas which is obtainable in different sized meshes from very fine petit point single-thread to coarse double-thread rug canvas. The working threads should be chosen to suit both the purpose of the embroidery and the scale of the canvas, and to design for any canvas work areas of colour and tone must be considered, rather than lines. Smooth and rough textures are obtainable with the use of different stitches, some being flat some lumpy. Broken colour is possible as some stitches such as rice stitch consist of two parts, each of which may be worked in a different colour and texture of thread; another way is to work each stitch with two or three different coloured threads in one needle, as by this method a great deal of variation is obtained using very few basic colours but with different combinations of threads. As stitches may be worked horizontally, vertically and diagonally, this must be taken into account when fitting the shapes together. Geometric ones look well but thin horizontal or vertical lines tend to sink and fine points are not suitable for medium to coarse stitchery as they look clumsy when translated on to the canvas and tend to reveal the background fabric. Beads may be combined with canvas work, either massed together or scattered, if more richness of texture is required. By using one colour, variation in tone is obtained by altering the direction of stitch and if a shiny thread is used together with a dull one for working out some of the stitches, this is emphasized. (Pages 113 and 322.)

Cross stitch is associated with peasant embroidery and although it is one of the canvas stitches and may be used entirely for canvas work, it is a stitch with infinite application. It may be worked on any fabric as when the threads cannot be counted a fine canvas is applied to the material over which the cross stitch is embroidered, the canvas threads being withdrawn afterwards. In designing for cross stitch, areas of solid and broken pattern should be balanced giving both strength and delicacy; double running, satin stitch and other stitches may be combined with cross stitch when appropriate. Colour is better limited to a few or even one as the texture and broken quality of well designed pattern is interesting and gives an appearance of tone according to the closeness of the stitches, which for perfection should be crossed the same way throughout: cross stitch may be worked to be viewed from both back and front of the fabric. (Page 177.)

Darning is a favourite stitch seen on many near Eastern embroideries and is used both for pattern and background areas. There are several kinds of darning and as long as the threads of the fabric are easily countable this method of covering it with pattern is reasonably quick and very effective.

1 *Irregular darning* consists of stitches of uneven lengths worked horizontally or vertically, to fill the background or the designed shapes or both

background and shapes, as colour can be varied and the darning can be reversed in direction for each area. After the basic pattern has been drawn, the stitches may be painted in on the squared paper if an idea of the final effect is required, but this is not generally necessary.

2 *Pattern darning* Here the design consists in the variation between smaller and larger patterns which give the appearance of different widths of satin stitch. Any geometric shapes may be darned, the areas of longer satin stitch contrasting with those of smaller stitches, the number of threads of the fabric left between shapes, also contributing to the general effect. When finished there should be a balance between the darned patterns and the plain fabric. Pattern darning may be worked in separate motifs or almost cover the fabric. It may be in one colour and texture of thread or may be varied in texture and colour as long as the working threads will pull easily through the background and are of the right thickness in relation to the weave. If a design other than geometric is planned, in which shapes are filled in with pattern darning, they must be very simple or the result will be too broken up and the coarser the fabric, the simpler should be the outlines of the pattern.

3 *Damask darning* is alike on each side and the stitches are worked both vertically and horizontally. Carry out those going in one direction first of all, and work the others, which are at right angles, afterwards. (Page 234.)

Double darning is alike on each side and design for it should be in simple blocks or fitting geometric shapes, rectangular ones being more successfully embroidered as the method consists of running taken evenly over and under any equal number of threads, and on the return journey picking up the opposite ones, making areas of solid stitchery.

Darning on net is of early origin and was done in imitation of the elaborate Italian laces, on hand-knotted square mesh called lacis. There are two kinds of darning on net today, that worked on hexagonal net and that done on the lacis, worked on a square mesh which is now called filet net. A non-stranded thread is most suitable for this darning and although colours may be used in darning on net, self-colour looks better if the effect of lace is required as the variety of textures obtainable is sufficiently interesting without the addition of colour which tends to cheapen it. Black on white, or white on black is effective and coarsely worked pattern in thick thread is exciting, balanced by contrasting ones in fine thread.

1 *Hexagonal net* The design has two approaches which may be combined or used as separate ideas. In the one simple reasonably large shapes are designed, which may be connected or planned as separate motifs and are filled in with lace stitches, with heavy outlines which enclose fine patterns, tone being obtained in the openness or closeness of their spacing. In the other, the design is entirely linear but again using different thicknesses of thread, the shapes are often narrower and a flowing quality is obtained by continuity of outline which is useful in any net darning as the fewer the joins of thread, the better. In this outline net darning, the design is drawn freely and transferred in Indian ink to architect's linen. Squared paper is not necessary for net embroidery and any shapes are suitable for darning, as long as it is remembered that fine points look blunted when worked on a coarse net and straight lines become wavy, unless following the mesh exactly.

2 *Lacis* or *filet net* darning requires a different approach and the pattern is darned into the squares solidly, leaving the background open, so that the design gives a good silhouette against the mesh. Very fine detail is not possible and the threads used for the darning must be chosen to suit the size of the mesh, non-stranded linen threads or coton-à-broder both being suitable for this type of net. The design may be planned on squared paper with divisions to correspond with the mesh of the lacis or it may be drawn freely and modified in the working out. Detached patterns may be darned to give a lighter appearance in contrast to those of the more solid shapes. (Page 177.)

Drawn fabric work depends on a lace-like quality for effect and is worked on fabric with easily counted threads. This may be as fine as handkerchief lawn or as coarse as sacking. It was seen in Europe during mediaeval times, was introduced into England in the seventeenth century, and has remained popular until today. In self colour again, it can resemble a lace with the working thread disappearing into the background, using contrasting colours a different effect is obtained but there is no rule to restrict the use of colour other than the final appearance of the embroidery.

In designing for drawn fabric embroidery the shapes should be smooth and non-niggly as these are filled with openwork patterns worked on the counted thread of the background. This gives variety in tone according to the number and sizes of the holes made by drawing the threads of the material together. Some patterns give small textures and holes, some larger ones, while some parts worked in satin stitches give solid, smooth areas. Outlines were originally heavy but today they may be omitted. Strong threads such as linen or coton-à-broder of the same weight as those of the fabric are less easily seen and will withstand a certain amount of pulling, which is necessary to make the holes large enough. On the other hand, thick threads give a different and quite interesting effect if used for some drawn-fabric stitchery. They are not suitable for all stitches. (Pages 178 and 179.)

Drawn thread work is of peasant origin, and as the threads of the fabric are withdrawn, either vertically, horizontally or in both directions, the pattern must be based on straight lines and rectangular shapes, with the lengths and widths of these planned so that they are not too large to weaken the fabric by the withdrawal of too many threads together. Where a vertical and a horizontal band overlap there will be an open rectangle, which may be filled with embroidery, either as a wheel or with lace stitches, worked over inserted threads. By planning the design on squared paper, the balance of open and semi-open shapes, the widths of the bands of drawn threads and the amount of embroidery necessary on them to give the right weights in relation to the whole, is more accurately ascertained. The whole design should be considered in areas of tone, the darkest ones will have most threads removed, the lightest ones will consist of plain fabric on a light material,

but if black fabric is used the position is reversed. The amount of embroidery worked into the remaining threads, if self colour will also affect the tone. A freer and more spontaneous method of planning drawn-thread patterns is to block in the dark areas of the design first of all with paint or pencil and to indicate patterns of threads within these areas with a light paint, then to plan other stitchery around them. Or put a pale wash of colour over the paper first of all, and indicate stitchery and fabric in white paint and pencil on the wash. By tying bunches of threads together more open holes are made but embroidery can be worked into these holes to give a decorative quality and to strengthen the fabric. A slightly thicker thread than that of the warp is better for working patterns over the threads of the fabric, but a fine one which does not show should be used for hem stitching when required.

There are several types of drawn thread work with particular characteristics which affect the design. **Hardanger work** from Norway is one of these and is basically geometric in style. It is done normally on coarse linen in self-coloured threads with kloster blocks of uneven numbers of satin stitches arranged round open shapes from which some threads may be removed afterwards both vertically and horizontally leaving a network of threads into which lacy patterns varying in density may be worked. Surface stitchery and darning may be introduced in the design. The areas cut away give good tonal balance as against the solid stitchery, particularly if this is in self coloured thread, which for the satin stitch blocks should be thicker than those of the fabric, with the lacy patterns worked in finer threads. The groups of threads not withdrawn from the holes are covered with overcasting or made into woven bars, they may have picots and lace stitches worked into them, this means a careful drawing on paper to show the positions and widths of the bars and the patterns in the holes between them if an idea of the final effect is wanted. Small holes enclosed within groups of threads may be left without patterns in them and today many non-geometric designs are built up in Hardanger embroidery which has many possibilities.

Hedebo work is of Danish origin, has many variations, is usually worked in self-coloured threads, sometimes with metal ones added and on a coarse or fine linen or even on muslin. The design may be as freely interpreted as possible and of any type and consists in planning shapes from which threads are withdrawn, those remaining being worked in lace patterns, often in buttonhole stitch together with solid shapes in satin stitch, eyelet holes and surface stitchery. These are worked to form the heavier parts of the decoration to give a richly textured effect and should be considered always in relation to the open parts of the pattern, with lace-like fillings.

Russian drawn work Here the design is left as a silhouette in the fabric while background threads are withdrawn in groups, both vertically and horizontally, leaving a lattice-like mesh which is whipped diagonally to give a final coarse net-like appearance to the result. In designing for this kind of embroidery, the simplicity of the shapes is important. They should be well enough planned so that detail is unnecessary, they must be basically geometric and the mass of solid fabric against open mesh is important as the weight of the embroidered parts can look too heavy if sufficient material is not left plain. Thick outlines may enclose the shapes with open patterns worked into the lattice background if wished.

Needleweaving is of peasant origin and often used for the decoration of costume. Threads are drawn from the fabric in one direction only and embroidery threads are woven back into those left, to form patterns in blocks and bars. The design may consist of solid blocks of one or more colours or self colour, or of solid blocks with woven bars and whipped bars. The pattern may be designed on squared paper but a successful result is obtained by free planning of solid and open shapes, the solid ones being woven in first of all, the whipping of the single and bunches of threads being finished afterwards. If the design is to fit well together and is to be subjected to hard wear any groups of long single lines should be avoided or worked in with the solid blocks as they tend otherwise to separate themselves from the stronger parts. They should be interwoven and connected with the blocks as weaving progresses, not, in this context, worked separately. On the other hand for decorations which have to withstand little wear anything is permissible, long, thin bars, separated to give a cobwebby effect, or tied together to give areas of space as against those woven in solidly with threads of different texture which may be varied in thickness and colour. Geometric patterns are normally embroidered in this method and should be worked on a loosely-woven fabric with threads slightly thicker than those withdrawn, but today needleweaving on coarse fabric gives many aspects for experiment, using very thick thread such as chenille and slub yarns with which to weave the patterns.

Double running is a simple type of embroidery to execute and has been found on early sixteenth-century work. It is alike on both sides and consists of lines worked in running stitches which take up and leave an equal number of threads, the spaces being filled in on the return journey. Design for this type of embroidery is entirely in line and may be drawn freely or be worked out on squared paper, on which each stitch equals one square, worked horizontally, vertically or diagonally. One contrasting colour to the background gives the best results, either light on dark, or dark on light, the effect being one of lace-like delicacy, with lines planned close together or far apart, to give weight and tone to the design.

Cut work is of Italian origin and comprises several types, from the simple to the complicated, the plainest designs consisting of small holes without bars to link the shapes together, the most complicated consisting of larger cut-away areas than fabric, which are linked together with open-work and lace stitches. A finely woven cotton makes a suitable background, worked with unstranded threads.

In designing for any cut work it is important that there are no detached shapes or if there are that they are linked to the background with bars. By cutting the pattern in paper of a light colour and laying this on a dark one, the proportions of the open shapes are seen more easily. They should not be too similar or too equally spaced or a monotonous sameness will result. The tonal

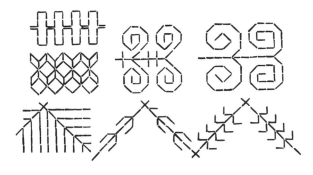

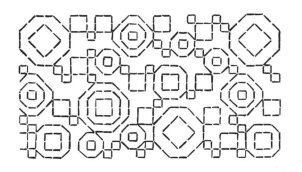

238 Double running patterns

holed or woven bars. When the main pattern has been planned successfully and cut in light coloured paper, stick it down to a dark background and draw in the connecting bars first of all with chalk; if they do not look right they can be erased easily. The thickness of the bars varies with the method of working them so that by placing these well, with different widths, the shapes are made more interesting and also variable in tone, in fact the successful planning of the bars so that the shapes are both strengthened and made more attractive is an important part in designing for this cut work, their pattern value being one of the chief characteristics of this type of embroidery.

(c) *Richleau work* is more elaborate than renaissance work in that the bars are decorated with picots which gives a more broken and lace-like effect. The cut shapes may be even larger than those joined by undecorated bars as the picots tend to fill up the spaces, especially on the wider, woven ones; they should be indicated in the design and grouped so that the result is not too fussy. Free-standing shapes are permissible in any cut work as long as they are connected by bars to the main ones, while sufficient openness in cutting shapes must be allowed, for contrast of tone between the fabric and the distribution of holes.

(d) *Reticella work* is the most elaborate form of cut work and similar to Italian embroidery of the fifteenth and sixteenth centuries. Larger areas are cut away than fabric remaining, sometimes squares are filled in with openwork patterns of lace stitches, mostly worked in buttonhole as in the needlepoint laces. Geometric patterns are particularly good for this form of embroidery as the complicated fillings are worked more successfully in the simpler shapes and they look more attractive. The basic planning may be variable in proportion and disposition, the buttonhole fillings being indicated on the dark paper shapes for working in self-coloured thread, thus quite altering the tonal effect by their closeness or openness of stitch. In carrying out this embroidery tack the fabric on to stiff paper, which will keep it from stretching and on which the patterns are indicated in ink lines giving a guide for the filling stitches. (Page 180.)

value of the pattern is obtained by the grouping of the holes and the distribution of bars which break up the cut shapes.

(a) *Simple cut work* As there are no bars in this work the cut out shapes must not be too large so that the background is weakened and there must be no unattached pieces. Narrow points are unsuitable as the edges of the shapes are whipped or buttonholed and the thickness of the working thread would make these clumsy at the apexes.

(b) *Renaissance work* is a more intricate cut work with larger shapes linked with whipped, button-

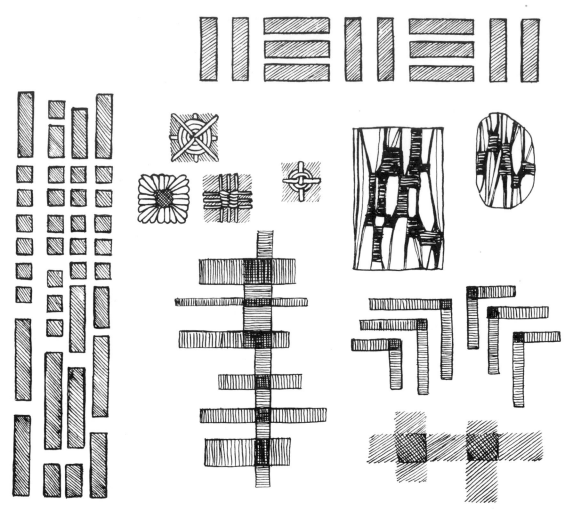

239 (a) Planning of drawn thread and cut work patterns on paper

Appliqué is one of the oldest types of embroidery known and is a means by which various fabrics are cut out and applied to a background of a different colour, tone or texture. In designing for appliqué it must be remembered that many materials fray so that shapes to be cut in them should be basically simple, without thin points which might disintegrate when sewing them down. Felt, leather and plastic are outside this rule and may be used to advantage in appliqué.

The work is better done on a reasonably large scale, with the preliminary design cut out in tones of coloured paper, the shapes being moved around until they look satisfactory in arrangement. These shapes can be pinned down to a paper background with the stitchery and threads indicated in chalk lines to give a better idea of the result being aimed at, and also used as patterns for cutting the applied fabrics. Colour and texture must be remembered in relation to tone which is easily

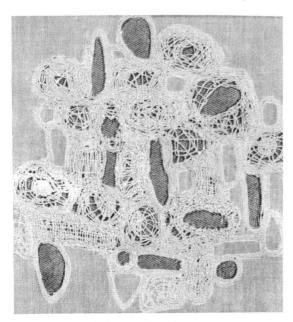

240 (a) *Cut work done on the machine*

240 (b) *Machine embroidery for dress decoration*
Goldsmiths

altered by the surface qualities of the fabrics chosen, so that pieces of material to be used in the final embroidery should be available when the design is being planned. Shapes may be cut which fit together like a jigsaw puzzle so that no background shows or they may be arranged as separate motifs connected with stitchery, or as vignettes of shapes with the surrounding background undecorated. Whatever type is required, the shapes and the tones of fabric may be emphasized or altered by the addition of stitchery. This is indicated in the paper design over the chalk lines, with paint or colour of some kind to show tone and density, or by superimposed shapes cut out in different papers to give the main areas of tones and threads. The chief point to remember is to keep a basic simplicity of shapes in the applied pieces of fabric, over which more shapes may be built up, finally emphasizing the forms in stitchery.

Blind appliqué has similar qualities in design to that of appliqué, in that bold, simple shapes are cut out in fabric, but here the raw edges are turned in and are firmly hemmed down to the background. This method gives a slightly rounded quality of edge with a suggestion of padding or raising of the fabric from the background. The design may be entirely in applied shapes without any embroidery thus eliminating lines, although these may be added if wished. Well planned blind appliqué using suitably designed shapes and carefully chosen fabrics is very attractive.

Patchwork is of as ancient an origin as appliqué but is different in that it consists of fabric shapes cut out from templates, which fit exactly into one another and are sewn together to form large all-over patterns without backgrounds. These shapes are usually geometric and often a complete piece of patchwork is created using one template throughout, such as a square, diamond or hexagon. The interest is obtained by making patterns in different tones and colours of fabric, arranged as repeats, so that the centre of a large piece of work might be light surrounded by a darker border, a grid pattern might be made in one colour, which would contain lighter or darker shapes within it to make complete smaller patterns, but the entire piece of patchwork may be made up from one or two interlocking shapes with pieces of fabric being mounted on card templates so that the fitting together of all of them is accurate.

This kind of patchwork may be designed to scale, on squared paper or built up geometrically according to the basic shapes and overall size.

Another kind of patchwork consists of motifs spaced on a plain background; these may be geometric, such as diamonds fitted together to make a star, they may be floral with the repeating shapes made from templates or they may be non-repetitive and then rather more like blind appliqué than patchwork.

In all patchwork the design depends very much on the distribution of tone, colour and texture of fabric and in the balance of light against dark shapes, in the juxtaposition of plain versus patterned and shiny versus dull materials. Rich fabrics should be used with rich ones, cottons and the normally washable ones being kept apart from them as the two types do not combine easily.

Patchwork in which any shapes may be fitted successfully together, is done by making a tracing on tracing paper of the whole design. This is cut up into separate shapes, each one becoming a template for a patch, marked with an arrow to indicate the grain for the placing of the fabric under it. The paper shapes are tacked to the right sides of the fabrics, which are cut out with the usual turnings, these being pressed back until the edges of the shapes fit exactly to those of the paper. The turnings are tacked down on to the wrong sides of the pieces of fabric and the patches joined together as for any other patchwork. The templates may be used again as they are just untacked when the fabrics have been sewn together.

A type of work called crazy patchwork is sometimes seen, usually a jumble of shapes and fabrics without regard to tone and colour. This work unless planned with care so that the balance is kept of large against small shapes, dark against light tone with some scheme of colour arrangement, is a waste of time and cannot be called design. (Pages 180 and 181.)

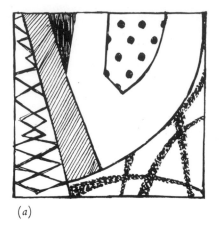

(a)

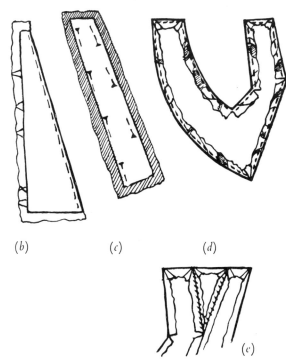

(b)   (c)   (d)

(e)

Seminole patchwork is another method, carried out by the Seminole Indians in Florida, where strips of material are sewn together by machine using several different colours. These are then cut up into small striped pieces of pattern and re-assembled to make new patterns of checks, crosses, diagonal patterns and others. Quite complicated results using a simple technique are possible, with these narrow strips of fabric.

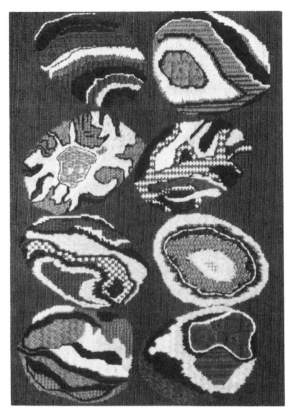

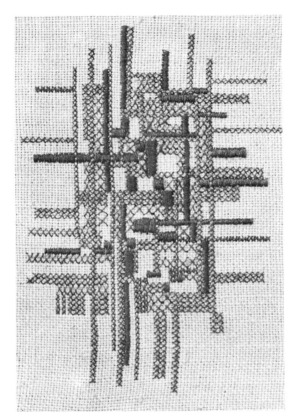

243 A canvas stitch panel with a design based on stones. The background is entirely covered with stitchery and is finely worked, the shapes being more freely interpreted in a variety of stitches. This design and method of work would be suitable for a stool top
Ann Shaw
Avery Hill College of Education

244 Cross stitch and satin stitch motif in blue on white. The crosses are worked to give a lacy appearance
Barbara Conroy

Opposite
242 Methods of preparing irregular patchwork shapes for sewing together
(a) irregular patchwork
(b) template on top of fabric—one edge turned in and tacked
(c) pinning template on to fabric, on right side
(d) wrong side of patch showing edge turned back and tacked
(e) patches oversewn on wrong side

245 Outline net darning, in coton-à-broder, raffine and anchor soft cotton. The motifs are taken from shepherd's purse and show different interpretations of the same subject

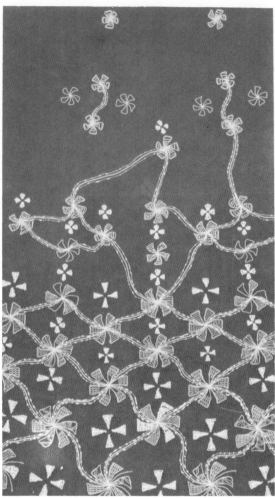

246 Part of a wedding veil darned on hexagonal net. This is unfinished, all the motifs are to be connected with trailing stems. Interest is obtained with solid and open darning
Molly Arnold

247 A wedding veil darned on hexagonal net. Repetition of a similar shape, differently proportioned gives a certain unity but also monotony
Goldsmiths

(a)

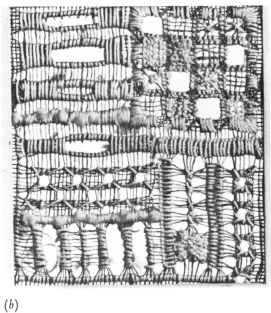

(b)

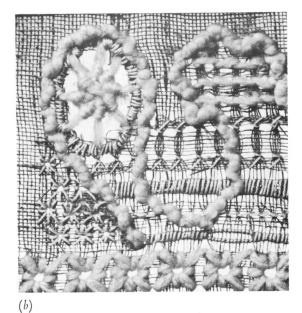

(b)

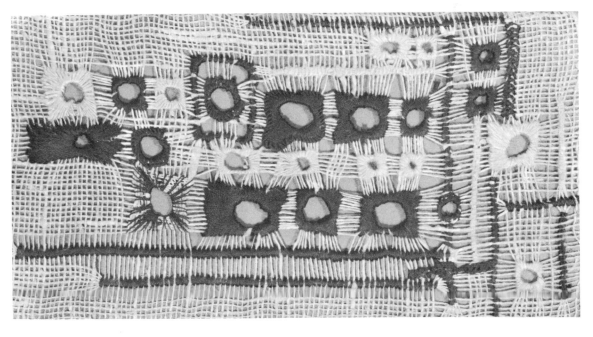

(c)

248 (a) *An example of drawn fabric stitchery showing variety of textures. White thread on grey linen*
(b) *Textures worked on scrim. Experiments for a pulled fabric decoration* Janet Sims
(c) *Eyelets clustered together* Cynthia Prentice

249 A cut work cover for a compact case

250 A similar design showing different types of cut work, with plain bars, whipped and woven, with picots and with buttonhole fillings   Kaye Norris

251 Part of a patchwork panel using a variety of shapes; based on a figure. Here the patchwork is used freely. The outlines were an afterthought and have not improved the design   Fiona Isbister

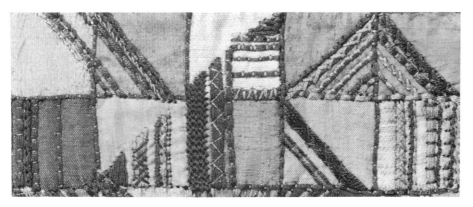

*252 A patchwork of squares of brightly coloured silks,
worked with embroidery   Isobel Chapman*

*253 Part of a bedspread in patchwork based on snowflakes.
The materials are entirely in blues and blue and white
patterned fabrics on a pink cotton background embroidered
in white threads   Mary Honeywood*

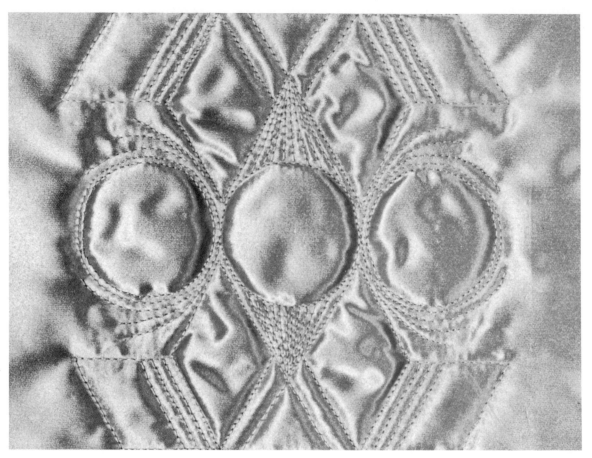

254 English quilting, part of a design on a bed jacket
Ann Preston

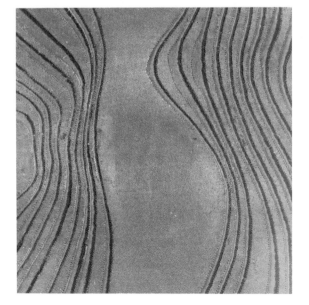

255 Italian quilting, worked on a machine with the rows of
stitchery threaded with fine cords and some wool
Diane Bates

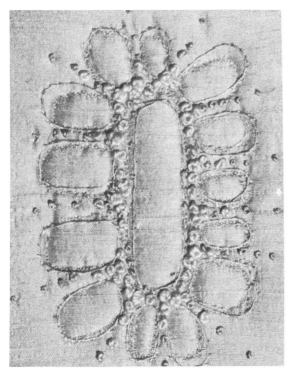

256 (a) Motif showing quilting and surface stitchery combined
Pauline Watson

256 (b) A motif using English quilting
Penelope Collins

257 Trapunto quilting in which the pattern is raised on a flat background
Goldsmiths

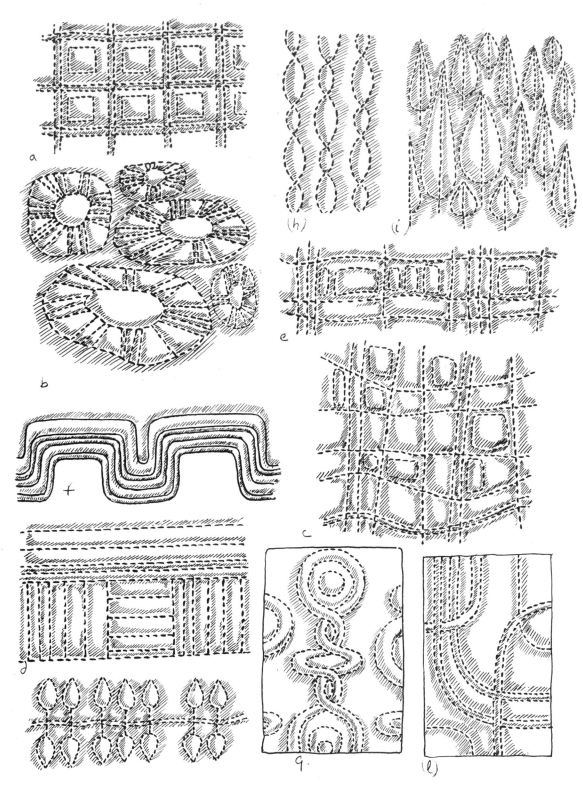

Shadow work is of peasant origin and delicate in conception. The embroidery is better worked on a fine fabric in non-stranded threads to suit the weight of stitchery required. The design should consist of shapes which are not more than 13 mm in width at the most unless the embroidery is for a wall decoration and has no wear, as the double back stitch or Indian shadow stitch used in working these has loose diagonal threads on the wrong side which could catch and be impractical if longer. Thin pointed shapes should also be avoided as they look clumsy as will too broken-up outlines, as the right side shows a back stitched line round each shape in the colour of the thread used. If the material of the background is transparent or semi-transparent the colour will show through, paler than the outline, if the material is opaque a slightly padded result is given by a little tautness of the under threads. Small geometric and abstract shapes, and those based on natural forms, may be effectively worked in this method, as long as they are uncomplicated. A form of shadow work done by machine may be designed with solid, brightly coloured fabrics stitched down on to the back of transparent fabric or between two layers of fabric, to give a more delicate appearance on the right side, with the machine stitching in white or coloured outlines. The sizes of the shapes may be variable as there is no hand embroidery in this work and the shadow effect is obtained with the applied fabrics. (Pages 100 and 158.)

258 Ideas for quilted patterns
English quilting
Italian quilting
Trapunto quilting
Italian and English quilting combined

Quilting has been used from the earliest times by all types of people, as it is a means by which two or three layers of material may be stitched together both for warmth and decoration simultaneously. There are several kinds of quilting, English, in which a layer of padding is placed between two fabrics, sheep's wool between linen originally; Italian quilting which is purely decorative and consists of an upper fabric backed with an openly woven one, with narrow band designs through which padding is threaded from the back to raise them, flat quilting in which two layers of fabric are stitched with narrow rows of pattern, then threaded with thin cords to give a decorative effect, and Trapunto also of Italian origin, where the fabric is backed in parts with a loosely woven muslin with small isolated shapes padded with animal wool.

English quilting traditionally done in South Wales and Durham, with local and characteristic patterns planned with templates, was mainly for warmth. This method of work has many exciting possibilities for design today, the aim being to keep the padding evenly distributed but at the same time to obtain variety of surface. In planning a design for English quilting, light and shade and an interesting surface texture may be obtained by areas of closely placed lines contrasted with those with little stitching, the latter unstitched parts will then appear to 'bubble' up as against the flatter closely stitched parts. Geometric shapes make a good basis for separate or repetitive patterns but as long as it is remembered that the whole idea is worked in single outlines of stitchery and that too many should not meet at one point as a clumsiness will result, any ideas may be tried out according to purpose. Two types of quilting may be combined if parts only of the article are to be padded and the whole of the outlines may be done by machine according to the intricacy of the design, or inclination towards hand or machine embroidery. Quilting and surface embroidery may be combined.

Italian quilting consists entirely of narrow bands or strips about 6 mm in width, planned as interlacing devices or as separate motifs. Geometric shapes are suitable as a basis for this type of design (avoiding fine pointed ones, as they do not thread easily) they may be made into bands or strips by a double row of stitchery and if tracing paper shapes are superimposed one on the other, interlaced patterns can be built up quite simply with the spaces between the ridges sufficiently large to prevent muddled threading with the padding. Continuous channels are easier to thread than very short ones so this is another point to remember in the design. It also avoids too many joins and bulkiness on the wrong side of the work.

A form of shadow Italian quilting may be done, using a transparent upper fabric, the channels being threaded with brightly coloured padding which shows through paler under the thin surface. It has a purely decorative value. It may be worked on the machine with the twin needle.

Flat quilting in which two layers of firm fabrics are stitched together without padding may be designed so that parts of the pattern consist of narrow parallel rows of stitchery—running being suitable for this, through which fine cords are threaded to give a raised surface where required. The rows look well stitched about 3 mm to 6 mm apart and whole areas of a complete design may be raised as against other areas of almost flat fabric. Curved shapes, simple geometric ones avoiding thin points and continuous lines are again easier to thread than the shorter ones and by massing the rows together in contrast to the parts left unthreaded a very rich effect may be obtained.

Trapunto quilting consists of a top layer with a thin under layer of fabric which is slit for insertion of the padded areas. The slits are herringboned or oversewn afterwards. The quilting consists of small areas of padding and is suitable for the decoration of dress when warmth is not necessary. Simple geometric spots, small leaf shapes and others based on natural forms are suitable for this kind of quilting, the shapes being planned to give a rich raised effect such as could be achieved with beads and jewels with surface stitchery and quilting combined. As each stitched area is padded separately it should not be too large in either direction as too heavily padded shapes look clumsy and become too isolated from the background fabric.

Embroidery using beads, jewels and sequins

is not of a particular type, but several points may be of help when using them in design. First of all they should be used generally on rich fabrics, although the non glittering china beads look well on cottons and woollens and the less elaborate textured fabrics. Beads should not be thinly scattered or they look anaemic, massed together they are exciting and the designs can be most easily planned when the main idea has been roughed in, by arranging the actual beads, jewels and sequins as required, within the drawn shapes. Graduation of size and shape gives interest, or the combination of beads and jewels or of beads and sequins; by moving them around, a good arrangement is found more quickly than by trying to draw them. There is a great variety of shape and size in beads, both glittering and dull, bugles of different lengths, faceted ones, smooth round ones, china and glass ones, while jewels can be smooth, cut into various shapes and very small, or quite large, up to 3.8 cm in width, and of innumerable shapes. They come in every colour, including gold, silver and pearl and much bead work is exciting, done entirely in self colour or in one contrasting colour but with different textures and surfaces and different sizes put together. Geometric patterns look well in beads but if whole areas are to be covered there should be some plan so that there is not an equal weight of pattern throughout. For elaborate evening wear, graduation from heavily massed to more open spacing, with sizes of patterns diminishing or increasing in proportion, gives interest, concentration on one part of a garment only such as the sleeves, bodice or hemline with other parts undecorated, gives emphasis where needed. Accessories may be jewelled while the garment remains undecorated, in fact there are endless ways in which beads and jewels may be introduced.

In ecclesiastical embroidery they can be used almost theatrically for vestments, hangings and frontals, combined with other rich embroidery such as padded work, metal-thread stitchery and with sumptuous velvets, brocades and heavy silks. For wall decorations small areas of concentrated glitter could be exciting in otherwise restrained designs and as long as the work does not become too weighty for the fabric, beads could be used as mosaics together with surface embroidery.

As the surfaces of most beads and sequins are shiny they will be affected by the play of light on them; this should be taken into account when choosing colours and shapes. Also their distribution and the articles on which they are sewn must be considered so that the right effect is obtained, either of strong theatricality or of discreet refinement. It is easy to obtain vulgar results, difficult to keep a balance of vitality and at the same time sensitivity, but well used, they are most exciting elements in embroidery.

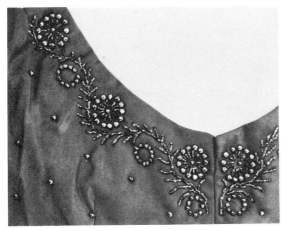

259 The neckline of a dress decorated with heavy Victorian beads bought in a junk shop

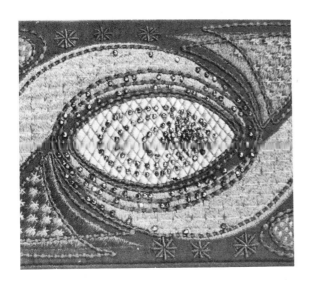

260 Part of a large hanging consisting of circles and parts of circles, couched in various thicknesses of wool in a number of colours. The tones are graded from strong ones in the centre to paler ones towards the edges and bottom of the hanging
Lynn Prosser

261 Part of the decoration on the flap of an envelope-type evening bag, in laid threads, with beads
Mary Harris

187

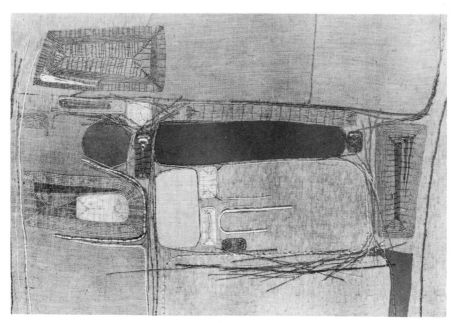

262 *A panel in couched strings, gold kid and cords, on hessian*
Josephine Windebank

263 *A selection of beads. There is a great variety and they have many possibilities*

264 *A very richly jewelled and beaded panel*
Anne Preston

265 *A detail*

265

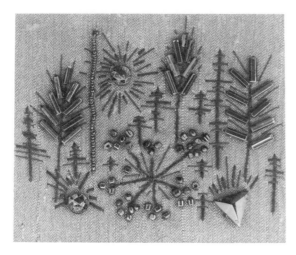

266 A sampler using a variety of beads   *Freda Tillott*

267 A white satin pin-cushion, with pins to hold down the sequins. In black with tatted edging   *Eirian Short*

Couching and laid work Couching consists in tying down one line of threads with another thread, which may be similar to or different from that being tied down. Laid work consists of a number of threads placed adjacent to one another to fill whole areas, kept in place with other threads laid across them, which are tied down with stitchery to create patterns; or groups of threads arranged with stitches tying down individual threads invisibly, or tied to make different patterns according to their placing. A shape entirely covered with laid threads has 'a laid ground'.

Designs for single lines of couching may be tried out in string and threads and if to be kept as permanent records may be arranged and stuck down on to paper or card. In the embroidery the thickness of the thread used and the method of couching will give character to the line. It may be very thin, such as one strand of stranded cotton, tied down with anchor soft cotton or perlita, it may be rug wool tied down with sewing cotton. The line may be variable, threaded with other threads at intervals to give thickness, the tying down thread being in strong contrast of colour and texture, or almost invisible and just a means of keeping the line in place. The result may be a broken effect or a very smooth continuous line, made up of one or several threads, the method of tying down and the threads used for this may be changed as wished on the same line and spaced regularly or irregularly according to the result required.

When areas are laid solidly with threads, the outlines of the shapes should be simple, the threads may be tied down individually and invisibly to create a smooth surface, they may be sewn down visibly the stitches being placed to make patterns or they may be overlaid in an opposite or different direction with other groups of threads which make patterns and are again tied down in some way. The design consists in knowing where the threads are to be tied down to form the patterns, how they are to be tied and the direction in which the threads are laid as this affects the final quality of the result with the play of light on them, otherwise as long as the basic shapes are simple, the same rules apply as for any other design.

A development of laid work is possible using padded areas, in which strings or felt shapes are placed under the threads. Here the design is planned so that any raised areas become the main point of interest. Small, smooth, raised shapes are obtained in a large area, by using felt in one or two layers, over which the threads are laid and sewn separately where they cover the felt, thus keeping them in place and giving the contrast between the flat and the padded areas. If string is used it must be placed opposite to the direction of the laid threads which must be securely tied down on each side of the raised ones as they encounter them. (Pages 65 and 225.)

Another method of working is based on the *San Blas Indian technique* for their molas. This is to place one layer of fabric over another with the pattern basted on the top layer. This is cut away in parts to reveal the under layer, turning in the edges with a needle and hemming these as the cutting progresses. Another layer may be between the top and bottom layer, so the second layer is cut and sewn as for the top layer. Applied pieces may also be added where wished. An advantage of this method is that sharper points are obtainable than with appliqué where edges are turned in. See *Art of Cutwork and Appliqué*, Herta Puls.

Inlaid work Here the background and patterns must fit exactly together like a jigsaw puzzle and both sides of the work are alike. Leather hangings were made in Spain during the sixteenth century, in this way. A non-fraying fabric must be used and the design should be kept simple. Counterchange patterns using two tones or colours in which the dark and light alternate, avoid any wastage of material, but providing that each shape fits exactly to the next, geometric and plant forms can be used. A point worth noting is that both positive and negative shapes may be made into two separate embroideries, the background or material in which the holes are cut will provide shapes for the other piece of material from which the insertions are taken. If more complicated inlay is required there is bound to be a wastage of material, although one of the disciplines in designing for this kind of work is to make sure that there is no wastage. The pieces are sewn together with a darning stitch or with a fine oversewing stitch.

Special Areas of Design

When planning embroidery for specific articles the suggestions for the building up of pattern from the simple to the complex, the choice of colour, distribution of tone and texture, are fundamentally the same, whatever the type of work involved. Each area has certain limitations which are a challenge to the designer, in ingenuity of planning and in solving the problem within the limitations imposed by the shape and nature of the particular article.

Before embarking on complete pieces of embroidery it may be advisable to experiment with unusual materials and unorthodox methods of work, to try out small samplers of combinations of textures and patterns, which are later incorporated in complete designs. Each experiment usually leads to another idea and a fresh approach, perhaps to a hackneyed subject, which in the end often produces the most exciting designs. Throughout all this remember that suitability of design and technique to purpose is the main consideration behind all decoration.

Dress

There is great scope for embroidery as a means of decorating dress, both for that of adults and of children. This area of study is very much tied up with fashion, at times lavish surface embellish-ment is in vogue, such as was the case during the reign of Elizabeth I, while at others, plain, un-adorned garments are worn, often due to economic stress, such as during wars or trade depression, when both money and labour are short and superimposed decoration an unnecessary expense.

From the wide selection in dress available there are a number of suitable styles which might be chosen and made more attractive with the addition of some embroidery. Although this form of decoration has always had a certain popularity in this country it is now used mainly for evening wear, when it is often jewelled, with beads and sequins lavishly employed, or with bold appliqué shapes or machine embroidery. On the Continent, embroidery is more popular on everyday garments and machine-embroidered blouses, dresses and children's clothes are very attractively decorated, while hand embroidery is reserved for the more exclusive models. The time factor tends to limit the amount of embroidery put on to any garment as too elaborate work, involving hours of labour, may result in the finished article being unfashionable even if the embroidery does not date, therefore this point must be considered when planning the design and in choosing the method of execution. A few other considerations will help when designing embroidery for any garment for an adult or for a child, these are:

(a) The purpose of the garment must be defined, whether it is for formal or informal wear, for day or for evening; from this is determined the choice of material most appropriate for the occasion and consequently the probability of it being laundered or cleaned. The embroidery must possess similar qualities to that of the fabric and if for children's clothes must be very durable. Machine embroidery is strong as it integrates with the fabric as does drawn fabric stitchery, but raised hand stitchery, couching, appliqué, beads and sequins are more suitable for the decoration of garments where hard wear is not involved.

(b) Embroidery applied to a garment should enhance both its value and its appearance and give it an exclusive quality, therefore the choice of style is important and such that its cut is appropriate for surface decoration, otherwise it is at variance with the garment and superfluous.

The decorated garment should have the quality of *haute-couture* rather than that of the 'arty-crafty' which is easily achieved with some kinds of embroidery; and although young people and children often look attractive in so called 'peasant' style clothes with brightly coloured stitchery on them, these styles are usually too unsophisticated for the more mature person for everyday wear.

(c) If the embroidery is for a particular garment for an individual whose main characteristics are known, the decoration may be placed judiciously to emphasize her best features, to attract the eye to one part of this garment, such as the neck line, waist or hip-line. There should be only one area of major interest on any garment, scattered pieces of embroidery on various parts of it lose emphasis and are best omitted, whereas a concentrated area of pattern gives richness and has purpose.

For children's clothes both the style and placing of the embroidery may be planned with possible alteration in mind, such as the letting out of fullness, the lengthening of hems or the application of false ones, without this being obvious.

In designing embroidery for children's clothes their ages should be known, as the scale of pattern in relation to that of the garment and the suitability of motif to age group must be considered.

268 A child's dress in orange furnishing cotton, decorated with simple stitchery on the three pockets   Doreen Elliott

269 A dress in blue Vyella decorated with numbers. Letters or geometric shapes could be substituted where appropriate
Ann Williams

A flower on the bodice of a dress for a three-year-old child might be quite swamping on a christening robe, while a toy engine which the same aged child would find attractive as a decoration on a pocket, would bore a seven-year-old. Patterns which stay in favour two years hence are more suitable, worked in an abstract context, such as circles, when the child may imagine that they are balloons, balls or whatever is wished according to age, and if altered later these garments will still appear suitably decorated.

Emphasis In concentration on a particular part of a garment there are a number of features, any one of which could be embroidered successfully, to give it individuality according to the general cut and style involved.

Embroidery may be planned to decorate:

(a) pockets, including flaps and welts,
(b) cuffs and sleeve finishes,
(c) collars and décolletage,
(d) fastenings such as buttons, buttonholes, belts and ties,
(e) darts and seams.

Besides these details, whole areas of garments such as the bodice, sleeves or skirt may be covered completely with embroidery, or an entire garment such as one for evening wear may be decorated from neck line to hem. It is a useful point to remember in planning embroidery for a whole garment that the result is more effective if the pattern graduates from close to open, heavy to light, from the hemline upwards or from the neckline downwards. This variation in weight of pattern avoids monotony and tends to flatter the figure besides evading exact repetition which would be tedious to work in hand embroidery.

Both the number of colours and the amount of pattern used is best restricted on adult day clothes as they can look garish or over elaborately decorated very easily. Pattern may be repetitive, consisting of embroidery built up in a variety of weights and types of threads, a combination of machine and hand embroidery or consist of non-repetitive motifs, isolated, or connected to form spot or all over patterns. Self-coloured embroidery or that related to the colour of the

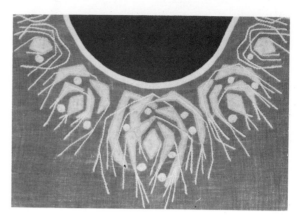

270 The neckline of a blouse decorated with applied double voile shapes, sewn with pin stitching. The design is floral, is strong structurally and 'non-arty'   *Kaye Norris*

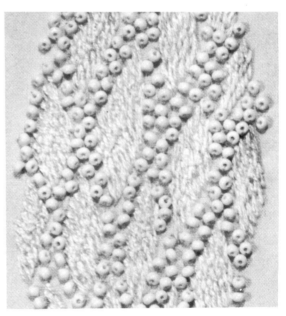

271 A small sample of embroidery in cretan stitch and white china beads, for an all-over decoration on dress. The pattern is based on the bark of the Spanish Oak

garment but in darker or lighter tones is successful, or stitchery in contrasting neutral colours such as white on black or navy, or in near neutral colours of cream or pale grey on white, or white on natural; none of these schemes glare and with the richness of the texture of the stitches are sufficiently interesting without several colours being used together plus the stitchery, which only gives a cluttered appearance.

For play clothes, leisure wear and informal occasions and for children's clothes more strongly contrasting and more brightly coloured embroidery is appropriate, with a freer approach to design, more use of amusing and unorthodox ideas and experiment in the combination of different materials with embroidery, as these clothes are not tied down by convention. In fact children's clothes give a greater scope for embroidery than those of adults, and the age range is such that designing patterns for the tiny child is quite different from designing embroidery suitable for garments for the young teenager. Any of these clothes for informal wear are attractive made of dark fabrics with embroidery in schemes of brightly coloured threads, such as slate grey denim embroidered in scarlet, yellow and blue, or in pink, orange and white. Narrow bands of stitchery, spots or other geometric shapes, letters and numbers are according to scale and arrangement, suitable for the decoration of garments for both adults and children.

Texture is an integral part of any garment and by combining two materials of contrasting textures, such as transparent with opaque as chiffon and velvet, or dull with shiny such as satin and wool, together with stitchery in self coloured threads, a very rich effect may be achieved. Very simple designs of well proportioned bands of alternate textures, or geometric leaf forms, circles or other basic shapes applied to a contrasting textured background and embellished with very little stitchery require careful planning but are most successful for formal decoration.

Another means of obtaining unity in embroidery on dress is to execute the decoration entirely in one stitch and preferably in one colour, such as chain or satin. Chain stitch or tambour work which was chain stitch done with a hook was practised in the eighteenth and nineteenth centuries and seen on Indian muslin dresses and later, with the invention of the Corneley machine, on thicker materials such as serge and face cloth where it was worked in self colour or in a strongly contrasting colour. By the concentration of close stitchery or by openly spaced lines a solid or lace-like effect was gained. Cable stitch done on the domestic machine gives a similarly effective result today and design may be planned in a similar way, with continuity of line.

Clothes for special occasions such as those for evening wear, or wedding gowns, may be very lavishly decorated as they possess a certain theatrical quality which means that the pattern may be bolder, the textures more in contrast and the colours brighter, when colour is employed. In fact, a certain amount of exaggeration is permissible, although this does not mean that the decoration becomes crude or garish in concept. If there is no emphasis the result may be half-hearted and timid, then the garments would be better undecorated. Richer and more obviously contrasting colours and textures are suitable for evening wear as both are influenced by artificial light and those which look well in daylight often lose their appeal under unnatural lighting. A variety of white textures can give a sumptuous effect and there are many different kinds of white, creamish whites and bluish whites which become emphasized in artificial light apart from their textures. China beads on cotton or muslin, pearls on wool, or thick cotton threads on satin and many other combinations of textures give infinite scope for design without colour. In considering the embroidered decoration for any of these rather theatrical clothes there is opportunity for unlimited creative outlet and extravagance which could result in exuberance or great restraint of style, in embroidery entirely covering a garment or in the decoration of an accessory such as a bolero or train or even a belt.

Embroidered accessories if well designed complement plain outfits. They are often small, and may be designed and worked as an introduction to the larger pieces of embroidery as they do not take too long to carry out, at the same time their overall shapes give an exercise in planning to fit confined or difficult areas, such as in designing patterns to decorate gloves or collars.

272 *Ideas for children's clothes. Lengthening hems, decorating seams, pockets, borders for various purposes. These are* basic *ideas which can be elaborated as needed and according to scale*

273 Ideas for distribution of pattern on accessories. Collars, cuffs, buttons, pockets, bags and belts. These are only skeletons on which more elaborate motifs are built up

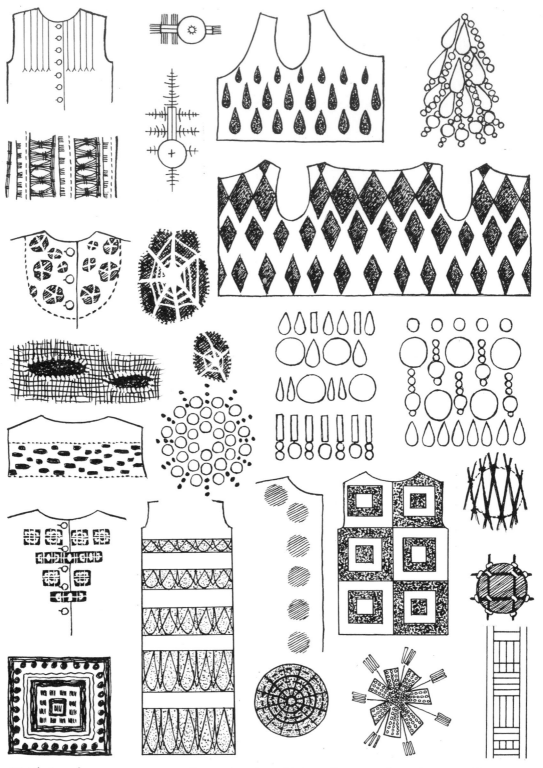

274 *Distribution of pattern on garments. Cut work and pulled work, suitable for hand or machine embroidery, buttonhole decoration, paillettes and beads semi attached to fabric, paillettes may be as large as half-crowns or $\frac{1}{4}$ in. in diameter, so according to size, very large motifs or quite small ones, may be built up*

275 *A border for a hair-band or a belt, using trapunto*
quilting and couched threads Ioné Dorrington

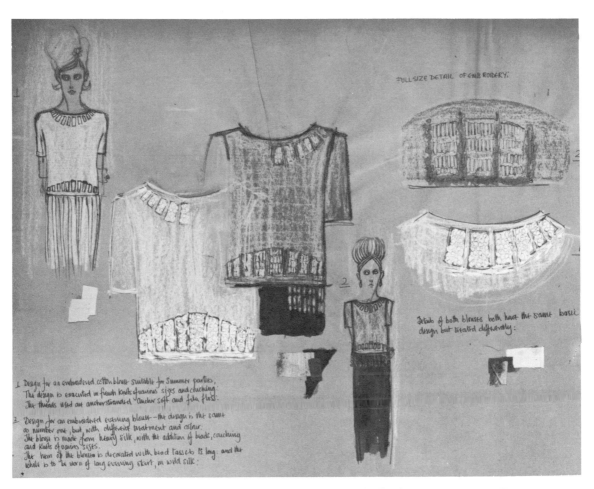

1 Design for an embroidered cotton blouse suitable for Summer parties.
The design is executed in french knots of various sizes and couching.
The threads used are Anchor stranded, Anchor soft and filo floss.

2 Design for an embroidered evening blouse — the design is the same
as number one, but with different treatment and colour.
The blouse is made from heavy silk, with the addition of beads, couching
and knots of various sizes.
The hem of the blouse is decorated with bead tassels 1½ long; and the
whole is to be worn of long evening skirt, in wild silk.

FULLSIZE DETAIL OF EMBROIDERY.

Detail of both blouses both have the same basic
design but treated differently.

276 (a) *Sketches for blouses, showing different treatments*

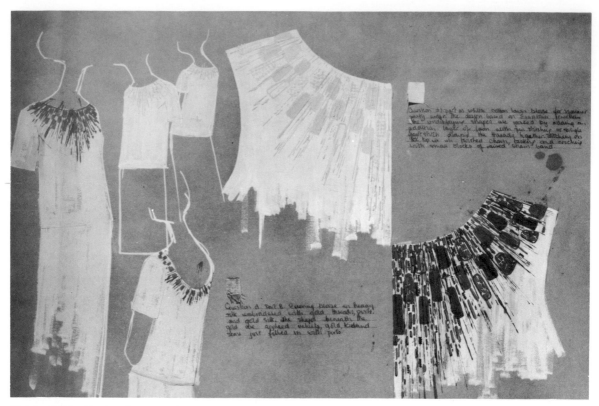

Question 3 part a: white cotton lawn blouse for summer party wear. The design based on Egyptian jewellery. The underlying shapes are worked by adding an addition layer of lawn with fur stitching or single feather stitch. Drawing the threads together, stitching on the top in twisted chain, raised and working with small blocks of raised chain band.

Question 3 part B. Evening blouse in heavy silk embroidered with gold thread, purls and gold silk. The shapes beneath the gold are applied velvets, gold, kidand leni just filled in with purls.

(b) Sketches for blouses, showing different treatments

277 Part of the decoration for an evening bolero, worked entirely in machine embroidery in self-coloured perle
Helen Sampson

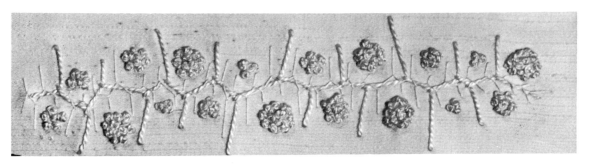

278 A border for a hair-band or a belt, using french knots
and cretan stitches   Pauline Watson

279 Part of a rectangular wedding veil with the two
narrower ends embroidered, in appliqué and stitchery with
silk threads on silk organza. Both sides of the embroidery are
viewable as the fabric is transparent and the veil makes a wide
scarf with the ends falling on to the shoulders. See fig. 60
                                    Mary Hilder

280 A hair-band in beads, sequins and threads

282 (a) An evening bodice of corded silk, worked entirely in cable stitch, using white perle and grey sewing thread. The motif is non-repetitive but basically a square or rectangular spiral   Susan Hathaway
(b) A detail of the bodice

281 The yoke of a woollen day dress, embroidered entirely on the machine in black and dark red threads and embellished with jet beads. The stitchery is done with a loose under-tension which gives a raised effect   Susan Wheildon

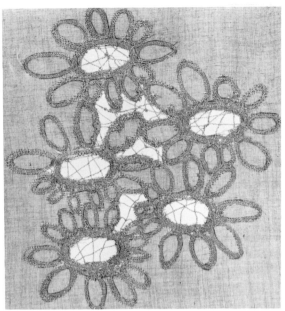

283 (a) *The daisy pattern embroidered more thickly in black thread on organdie*

(b) *The same pattern in white. These are first exercises but show lacy effect obtainable on fine fabric, also the different effect seen by changing the tone values*

Carol Jackson

284 *Machine embroidery on black organdie mounted on a bright crimson red silk, through which brilliant spots show in the cut work* *Sally Thompson*

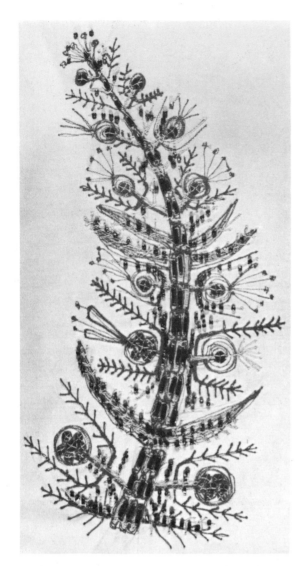

287 *Borders suitable for striped fabrics*   Goldsmiths

285 *A machine embroidered spray, richly embellished with beads of various kinds, for the decoration of evening wear*
     Goldsmiths

286 *Border pattern using unusual materials*
     Ioné Dorrington

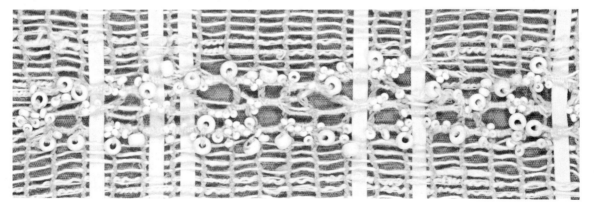

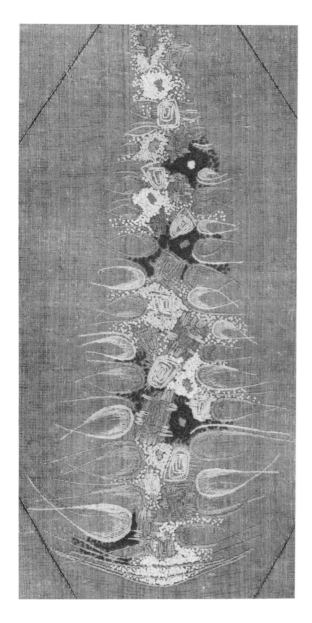

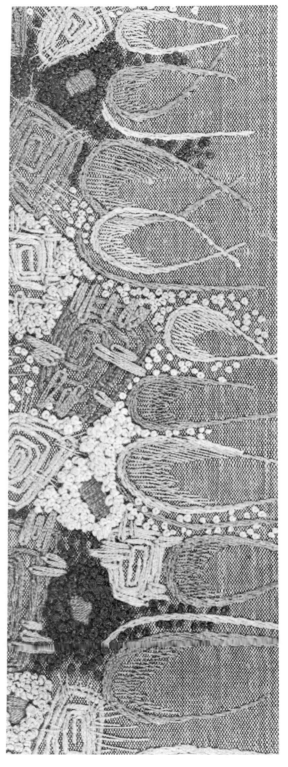

288 A panel of fine silk embroidery, which decorates the
skirt of an evening dress. On wild silk in greys, creams, dull
yellows and browns   Ioné Dorrington
   A detail of the embroidery showing the use of various
stitches, mainly cretan. The tones are muted and without
strong contrasts. The idea is based on drawings of shrimps

*289 Part of the embroidery on a bolero-type bodice, in blues
and greens on light navy silk   Mary Harris*

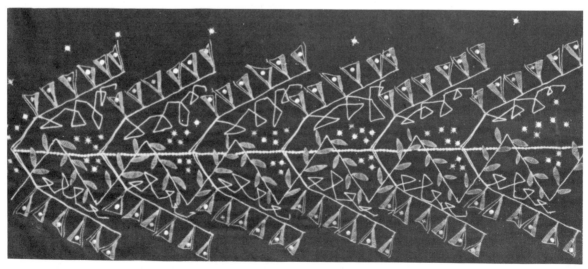

*290 A border in shadow work on nylon organza. Here the
repetition of triangular and oval leaf forms gives a unity
and an all-over effect   Diana Thompson*

Embroidery for the household and interior decoration

A wide use of embroidery is in the home, but the number of decorated articles in one room should be limited, otherwise there is confusion of style and taste and too much pattern creates restlessness. One well-planned piece of embroidery designed for a definite position in a particular room gives more impact than several haphazardly scattered pieces of work, placed independently and without consideration, in the same room.

Wall hangings and embroidery for the household must be suitable for cleaning or laundering, and there are several limitations which will be useful to remember when planning embroidery for household purposes.

(a) The importance of the article in the room must be considered. This article may contain the only areas of strong colour or may be the one richly patterned piece of decoration in an otherwise plain setting. On the other hand it could be one of several similar embroidered articles, such as cushion covers, chair seats or table mats, where the repetition gives less impact than the single piece of decoration but creates a certain unity of purpose.

(b) The type of room and its size in relation to the embroidery to be placed in it, is important, as this will determine the scale of decoration and that of the article in relation to its purpose. A lampshade for a standard lamp in a sitting room would be of a different scale from one for a bedside lamp in a small bedroom, consequently its decoration would be quite dissimilar in size. Embroidery for household accessories, in general should be designed to blend with the atmosphere of the room, unless it is to give the one vital splash of colour and pattern to it.

(c) The predominant style of furnishing, whether period or modern, or of no particular trend, the main colour scheme and other decorative features must all be taken into account when designing any embroidery which is to fit successfully into its surroundings.

Wall decorations have from pre-Christian times been carried out in embroidery and today are very popular, either as framed panels or free hanging decorated fabrics, which may be flat or draped on the wall according to the design. They may have a little or a great deal of stitchery, or they may be transparent with decoration viewed from either side, used as room dividers rather than against the walls. There is a great variety of approach in designing for these panels and hangings, incorporating all manner of materials and threads, from fabric collage to pure embroidery.

Collage has great popularity at present and might be included as a method of wall decoration, although it is not embroidery and possesses no skill as such, but it is a method of making decorations using absolutely anything that is wished, such as fabric, glass, metal, wire, stones and anything else which suits the idea. Designing collage is a good means of learning to plan shapes, textures, tones and colours together, as the basic rules for design to fill a given shape apply here if the collage is to be a success. When the various materials have been chosen, assembled and planned and the result is pleasing, they are stuck on to a background of fabric or whatever is wanted; metal, plastic, card or wood, but with fabric collage most of the design is made in fabrics stuck or sewn on to a fabric background. The decoration may be complete without further embellishment but threads and embroidery are sometimes added to give interest to the textures already used and also help to give a strength and security to the stuck down pieces. Most collage must be framed as it is not sufficiently durable to withstand any wear, but it has value as a design medium and as an experimental approach to the understanding and use of a great many different kinds of materials, and gives a broader outlook on all aspects of two-dimensional work containing apparent depth.

The technique for most wall decorations is related largely to purpose, a huge hanging would be better carried out mainly in appliqué or blind patchwork, in order that the larger areas of design are more quickly put down; while intimate decoration for a small hallway in a modern flat might be worked entirely in stitchery to give a rich, jewel like appearance. Fabric naturally hangs, but framing and glazing may be determined by the size of the work and the inclination of the designer. With framed and glazed embroidery much looser techniques are permissible as these are protected by the glass or are rigid; but for hangings, techniques used should be more durable as otherwise the threads and materials tend to loosen and become tatty. There is great freedom in choice of fabrics and threads, in the use of unusual materials which may be applied such as in the past when tree bark, shells, stones, metal and glass were in favour. These, however, needed to be incorporated with restraint and understanding or the final result looked 'cheap and gimmicky'. Dyes, manipulated fabrics, paper and paint, are more fashionable incorporated into hangings today. Non-fadeable materials should be used but any textures may be put together, such as sacking and velvet, kid and linen, provided that the overall effect is good and contains a unity.

Subjects for design depend on personal interpretation and the requirements behind the designing of the panel, fashion and ultimate destination. It is important to be aware of current trends in painting and graphic design, but not to copy them, as in embroidery qualities are obtainable which are impossible in other mediums; on the other hand it is easy to carry out purely illustrative embroidery, to obtain effects of reality which are better done in other ways such as with pen and ink or paint.

In designing a wall decoration the same rules apply as in filling any given area with pattern, the subject matter, whether abstract, geometric or based on natural forms is of first consideration, after which the area of chief interest should be determined. It may be that most of the background is to be undecorated, the position of the embroidered parts is then of greater significance, it may be that almost all the background is to be covered, but if this is equal in intensity of colour and proportion of shape throughout, the result will be uninteresting. When the idea is assimilated the main shapes are best cut out in paper, whether the embroidery is to be carried out in appliqué or to be worked in outline or solid stitchery. By using three tones of paper, black, grey and newspaper on a light background, or grey, newspaper and white on a dark background, the

areas of dark and light tones are more easily seen. This is a considerable help in working on a large scale as tonal distribution is as important as colour if the result is to contain vitality. It is also a help to work vertically on a wall as it is only in this way that the complete balance of shapes is seen as it will be when the embroidery is finished, and they can be moved around and re-cut if not correct, either in shape or in placing or in tonal values.

Techniques and materials may be mixed, with padding and pulled work used together, appliqué and cut work, machine and hand embroidery, silk, string, cords and wools, feathers, coarse with fine fabrics, thick with thin ones. Some experiment is needed to determine what effects are obtainable when using different combinations of textures and fabrics but this adds to the interest and excitement when designing in this field of embroidery.

If the embroidery is to be hung and not glazed, part of the design consists in the method by which it is hung, whether it is to have a particular finish such as a fringe, tassels or loops, whether it is to be hung with cord or with a rod slotted at the top and bottom through casings on the back, or whether tabs are to be incorporated in the final idea. The hanging may be non-rectangular and could be slung on strings to a metal surround or frame, it could be placed within an open framework and slung tautly by stretching it to the top and bottom parts of the frame. More than one strip of embroidery could be placed within one frame, in fact there are numerous ways in which the work may be hung but this must be decided when planning the embroidery as it should be a part of the complete design. The method will be determined by the purpose and position of the decoration as it might be flat against the wall or hung in folds or free hanging or even recessed, or it may consist of two layers of decoration, one behind another.

Household linens include bed linens, table linens and towels which launder, the embroidery must be durable and part of the fabric, hence the popularity of pulled work which strengthens and decorates the materials at the same time. Machine embroidery is suitable for the decoration of all articles in this category, but the result is richer if hand embroidery is combined with it. Overall shapes and purpose are limited to give a test of design within strict measurements and using a narrower range of background fabrics.

Decorative corners with borders, borders alone, initial letters and monograms, separate motifs or continuous patterns are all suitable for bed linen and towel decoration. 'Linen' is not strictly true now as cottons, nylons, terylenes and other synthetic fabrics are being used, plain or patterned, white or coloured so that embroidery in self colour or in contrasting colours is applicable.

Quilts and bedcovers are included in this field of decoration, and are exciting as design areas if large scale decoration is enjoyed rather than working to the smaller scale of initial letters. This does not preclude the fact that lettering may be large—it could be used successfully on a double bed sized cover or on a child's cot cover. In designing embroidery for both quilts and covers, there may be an up and a down or the patterns may be viewed successfully from any angle, according to inclination. Quilts are mainly for warmth and therefore are padded throughout, the three layers of material being sewn down with patterns planned as geometric repeats, as uneven abstract shapes or as complete decorative units without repetition. Remember in designing for quilting that the padding must be kept in place, therefore a too large area must not be left unstitched, at the same time, the balance between plain and worked areas must be kept if the result is to look interesting, the tightly stitched and flattened parts contrasting with the bumpy and unstitched ones. Stripes, borders, central motifs, spot motifs with subsidiary patterns worked round them are all ways in which designs suitable for both quilts and covers may be built up. In embroidering a bedspread or divan cover there is no limitation in technique other than that if appliqué is used for the decoration it must be sewn down strongly, blind appliqué and patchwork motifs are therefore good ways in which design may be carried out; also the embroidery need fill only a small area as against the complete area of a quilt. Pillow

covers into which pillows are slipped during the day may be embroidered to match the cover or quilt, with scaled-down designs or with parts of the larger designs selected to suit the smaller areas.

Table linens include table cloths of various sizes, table mats, napkins, tray cloths, runners, tea and coffee cosies; in a variety of shapes, square, rectangular, circular and in the case of cosies, semi-circular, dome-shaped, box-like or of any shape suitable to fit over tea or coffee pots.

Machine embroidery is suitable for the decoration of these articles as it is durable. To give it more weight it may be combined with hand embroidery but both should be of the flat type as raised stitchery would not support plates well. Darning and counted thread patterns are strong and consequently popular but may be combined with other types of stitchery to give more interest to them, to avoid monotony in working out, and to encourage the combination of various techniques.

All table linen is used in conjunction with china, cutlery and food and therefore colour should be limited, also the disposition of patterns, as mentioned previously. It should be planned broadly before details are decided as there are less obvious ways in which pattern may be distributed other than with borders. Neither does the overall shape have to be of the conventional rectangle or circle, as long as its purpose is kept in mind. The cloth may be for everyday use or it may be for special occasions such as wedding ceremonies, banquets, birthdays or festivals when it may be decorated with appropriate symbols or lettering. The same points apply when embroidering place mats or tray cloths but much of them is covered when in use, so that pattern needs to be limited in amount and in distribution.

Tea and coffee cosies besides looking attractive must be sufficiently large to fulfil their purposes. Again colour should be limited but there are several approaches to designing for them as they may consist of loose covers, transparent or opaque, over quilted linings, or may be completely quilted, or a combination of surface stitchery and quilting.

Decorated household accessories consist of articles on which decoration is not essential but if well designed can add greatly to their individual characters and to that of the room in which they are placed. Within this range are cushion covers, lamp shades, curtains, pelmets, stool tops and chair coverings, also embroidered rugs; some articles being subject to hard wear while others, although functional, receive little wear and tear.

Cushion covers may be of any shape, subject to hard wear or purely decorative. They should be viewable from any angle if square or circular and in designing patterns for them it is useful to know if they are to be repetitive units in a room or individual both in pattern and colour.

There are opportunities for effective decoration of lamp shades which receive no hard wear but should look equally attractive lit or unlit. Background fabrics may be semi-transparent or opaque, any type of pattern is suitable, providing it is compatible with that of the overall framework; eyelets and drawn fabric or drawn thread embroidery in part would provide openwork through which the light could gleam at night. Small area of brilliant, thin silks could be inlaid on dark, opaque fabrics giving a mosaic like appearance and both shadow and cut work, appliqué, and heavy stitchery are techniques suitable for design which is seen under variable conditions. Machine stitchery on nylon or organdie, combined with openwork gives a delicate, cobwebby appearance suitable for the smaller lampshade.

In decorating curtains the size and the amount of pattern is of first importance. Notes on the designing of hangings could apply here, but curtains are usually made to draw back or to cover a window or door and should look effective in either position. Too stiff fabrics and large unyielding shapes should not be employed as they might on a hanging used purely for decoration. Net curtains and room dividers in fine fabrics in which both sides of the articles are seen, look well embroidered by machine, or with transparent applied shapes, some on one side of the curtain, some on the other. Patterns on these would never look obtrusive owing to the fine nature of the fabrics used, although they could be dyed to

rich dark shades and embroidered in blacks, purples and dark reds, blues, or in combinations of any deep colours.

Embroidered pelmets may be used with plain curtains, in which case they will stand elaborate decoration, but being shallow in depth the design is limited to a border or central motif, although a shaped lower edge calls for ingenuity in planning. As the pelmet is above eye level, sometimes quite highly placed, a bold, simple pattern is suitable, in appliqué, inlaid work or in couched cords or heavy threads to emphasize lines rather than solid shapes.

Canvas embroidery is an obvious method for working stool stops and chair coverings as it is hard wearing and may be bold or delicate in concept. Geometric and abstract forms, repetitive and individual non-repetitive patterns, formalized natural shapes are all suitable for design, although experiment should be made to find out which stitches wear best before selecting those most applicable to the patterns to be worked. A stool top should be planned to be seen from any angle but a chair has a back and a front and the design should be placed accordingly. In designing

291 A tea cosy, using cow parsley as a motif, on a grey green background, worked in black and white threads

Anne Preston

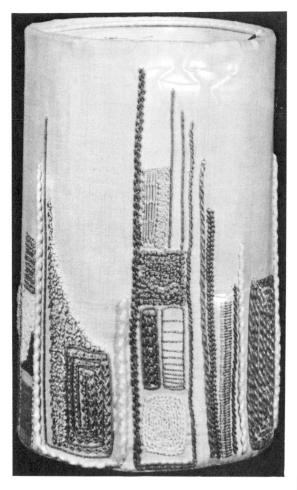

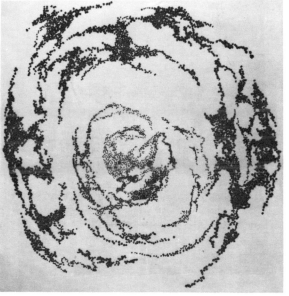

292 *A lampshade embroidered in heavy stitching on fine white fabric* Goldsmiths

293 *A cushion cover of orange wool with embroidery combining quilting and various stitches, worked in reds, orange, pink and white threads* Kathleen Hoskins

294 *Design carried out entirely in french knots. Suitable for cushion cover or wall hanging according to scale* Brenda Holmes

295 A panel—small motifs on a black background. Plain and patterned fabrics are combined. Overlaid with black organdie

Surface stitchery is worked over some of the patterned fabrics to give emphasis
Ursula Gillette

for embroidered rugs the same points apply, although the work is on a coarser scale and the stitchery bolder. The rug should be complete in itself, not looking as if it had been cut off by the yard from a repetitive patterned fabric, in short it should be planned to fit the particular shape and area and to suit that of the room.

Other household articles are no doubt suitable for embroidery decorated to suit individual requirements.

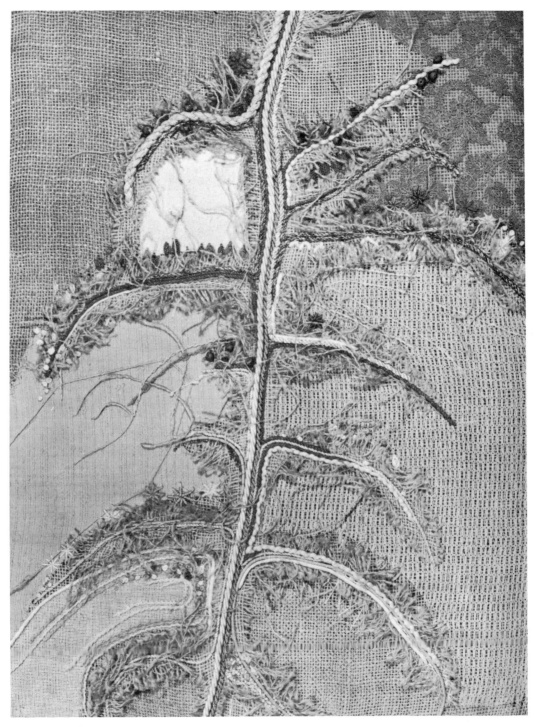

296 'Fern'—a panel in which the frayed edges of the fabric
give the main interest   Anna Wilson

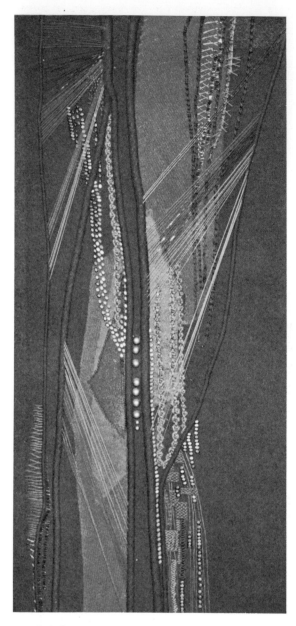

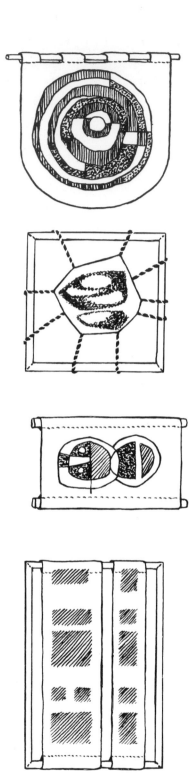

297 'Black and bronze'—a panel using cords, overlaid
with raised threads, and large beads   Beryl Chapman

298 Methods by which hangings may be suspended, framed
or hung loosely
(a) with tabs or a rod
(b) suspended freely on cords
(c) with slats threaded through hems

299 Two separate panels hung on one frame

300 A panel depicting the 1960s in appliqué in reds, greys and oranges. See figure 61   *Isobel Hare*

Ecclesiastical embroidery

The same rules apply as in designing for other forms of embroidery, its purpose, background setting and particular services with which is it associated, must be known before working out ideas. Specialized information is obtained from books dealing exclusively with ecclesiastical work.

Colour has always played a symbolic role in the church and although the liturgical colours are not now always strictly adhered to and some are variable in their usage, there are times when certain colours are appropriate, such as white for Easter, or white and gold for festivals and weddings, blue, grey or violet for Lent and Advent, while dark red, purple or black are associated with Good Friday, and green with Trinity. Red which may be scarlet or crimson is symbolic of Whitsuntide and the Feasts of the Martyrs. Here again much more information on detail may be obtained from specialized sources.

The architectural setting is very important as the embroidery must suit this, whether it is eleventh-century Norman and solid but simple, fourteenth century decorated with elaborate detail or modern and quite stark but beautiful in a different way. The scale of the building which may be large and impressive or small and friendly as in a country church must be considered in relation to the scale of the embroidered decoration, as the larger the church the bolder the design so that it may be seen well from a distance. The decoration on a frontal in the smaller building would be much less imposing than that for a high altar in a cathedral of large dimensions. The decoration of vestments must be designed with a similar awareness of scale.

Symbolism plays an integral part in church embroidery, it is a fascinating subject and the basis of much ecclesiastical design and should be studied in detail when undertaking specific commissions. The cross, the circle and the triangle, birds, fishes, the sun and moon have been used from the first days of Christianity as symbols of the Faith and before that as pre-Christian symbols, the tau of Egyptian antiquity being the forerunner of the cross as it is now known. They are today still some of the most exciting elements of design. Heraldry is another basis of church decoration and heraldic embroidery when appropriate is very effective as it must be bold and well planned.

Embroidered decoration for the church should possess dignity and a basic simplicity although it may be very rich in feeling, while the technique and stitchery must suit the size of the design. Generally in the past, the decoration was evolved to tell a story to the illiterate populace. It was very fine in technique, including manuscript illustration, wall paintings, stained glass and sculpture, and embroidery had a pictorial quality not necessary today; therefore symbolic, geometric and abstract shapes are an appropriate means of adornment as well as the use of figurative subjects. Appliqué is an ideal method of decorating hangings and panels and when carefully applied and secured with overlaid stitchery is sufficiently strong for vestments which are worn constantly. New churches often possess free standing altars, when frontals are unnecessary, but simply decorated drapery is effectively used.

Frontals and hangings Large areas may be covered with embroidery, or there may be central or isolated motifs on undecorated backgrounds. A feature of all this work is that it must 'tell' from a distance; the silhouette of the pattern is important as an idea to be grasped quickly on entering the building.

Any subjects are possible for interpretation, the well-known ones such as the cross, the rayed sun and the symbols of the apostles and various saints are always a good basis for design. The areas may be divided up as for any hangings, with symmetry or asymmetry. Colour may be dictated by the use of the embroidery for particular festivals, and even this is arbitrary. It should give simple but bold contrasts of tone and the larger the building, the stronger this should be.

Banners usually incorporate a certain amount of lettering such as the name of the Guild, Mothers' Union or the Saint to whom the church is dedicated. Letters have considerable decorative qualities (see page 229) and in their own right are sufficiently exciting to be used alone, although they are seldom seen without other motifs. In designing for banners it must be decided whether they are to be carried in processions or are to remain stationary, as those to be carried often have both fronts and backs decorated, the former with the symbols the latter with lettering. Decoration for any banner should be simple and clear cut without unnecessary, fussy detail, so that its meaning is immediately understood and lettering should have pattern value as well as legibility. The overall design of the banner incorporates the method of suspension and finishing of edges as these can make or mar the completed article and must have some relationship to the decoration if to be successful.

The same simplicity applies in designing *pulpit falls* and *lectern covers*, they must be sufficiently large in size to suit the furnishings, with the pattern planned to avoid 'bittiness'. A cross has so many variations both in its type and in its design possibilities that it is an excellent basis for any ecclesiastical pattern.

Kneelers, book and seat cushions are best designed to be worked in canvas stitchery and more unity is given if a basic colour scheme is used throughout a building, which picks up that of the stained glass, the colours of the stone, woods or metals incorporated in its construction and furnishings. Again symbolism and lettering are appropriate means of decoration and heraldry may be used successfully, with its strongly contrasting but limited application of colour.

Altar linen The embroidery design should be simple. On the *altar cloth* the design is usually in the form of small crosses carried out in white stitchery. It must wash, therefore durable stitchery is necessary and a combination of hand and machine embroidery is appropriate. The *burse*, approximately 23 cm square, may be richly embroidered, in metal threads and silks, in any colours and with any motifs and is better if designed to be seen from any angle although it may have a top and a base. It must be lined with white linen, whatever material is used for the outside cover. The *chalice veil*, 51 cm × 61 cm square, is made of the same fabric as that of the burse and is similarly decorated but often on the edge which falls over the front of the chalice.

Vestments are decorated according to their purposes, for festivals and special occasions very elaborately, but for everyday services simply and with little embroidery. The *cope* is used for special festivals and in certain processions. It is an almost semi-circular cloak, stiffened and of a sumptuous appearance, this being obtained with the materials used and in the richness of the decoration, which lends itself to elaborate embroidery with the use of silks, gold and silver and other metal threads, pearls, jewels and beads, together with applied fabrics, kid, velvet, brocade and anything with quality. To use cheap materials would be a waste of time for any ecclesiastical embroidery. The centre back is the most important area of decoration, from which the rest of the design may radiate, but it must be placed carefully so that the pattern hangs correctly over the shoulders and down the centre fronts of the garment. The cope may be entirely covered with embroidery, heavier towards the hem, or more thickly worked on the shoulders, or may consist of a repetitive pattern or of a central motif from which subsidiary ones radiate. It may have an embroidered orphrey and a plain or a decorated hood, and fasten with an embroidered morse. With the cope an embroidered mitre is usually designed, to be worn with it, the decoration being in the same vein as that of the cope.

The *chasuble* hangs softly and drapes with less elaborate decoration but again it depends on the ceremony for which it is worn. This garment has assumed various shapes during the past, but it is essentially an oval or almost circular garment covering both front and back of the figure, without a front opening but with a hole for the head placed slightly more towards the front of the shape than to the centre. The design is often on the back of the chasuble only, or is more elaborate on the back with a little decoration on the front. The fact that it drapes should be born in mind when designing, also that shapes and lines are better if upward sweeping, in order to avoid a depressing appearance when the arms are down. Simple, bold shapes, appliqué and blind patchwork without stitching may be effectively used on the chasuble.

The *alb* is decorated with apparels on the cuff and hem, these being bands of embroidery in white or in colour usually designed to go with the robes. The *amice* has an embroidered apparel about 7.6 cm deep and 56 cm long and is detachable for laundering. The *dalmatic* and *tunicle* are each decorated with two vertical bands or clavi and with two horizontal apparels on the front and two on the back of each garment, one near the neck and one near the hem. These may be of any appropriate colours, and look well designed on a geometric basis. Machine embroidery is suitable for the decoration of these bands.

Stoles and *maniples* are worn with the vestments of the appropriate colours to go with them.

They are often decorated at the ends only, but may have separate motifs on their entire lengths of approximately 244 cm to 274 cm with a width of 7.6 cm. Again symbolism is appropriate but should be kept simple in conception on this small scale or the result is finicky. A stole is a good article for design when commencing to do ecclesiastical embroidery and gold work, as a small area only need be decorated and ideas tried out which must be basically simple, involving elimination of unnecessary detail.

Further specialized information on church decoration, symbolism and ecclesiastical embroidery may be obtained from books listed in the bibliography.

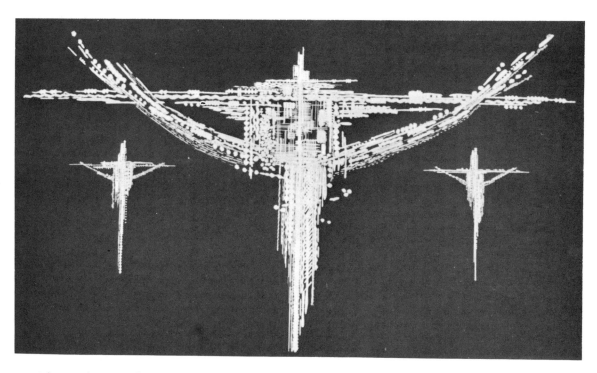

301 The central portion of an altar frontal portraying The Crucifixion embroidered in a variety of white threads on a red background. The effect is one of refinement but has rich textures giving apparent depth　　　*Gillian Hall*

302 An altar frontal in greens and purples, with an intricate design based on crosses, both symbolic and ingenious as the circles also represent the Trinity   Isobel Hare

303 An altar frontal in purple, blue and black, one of a set of four designed for the Chapel of the Deaf, the Alban-Neve Centre, Luton. Here lettering is used as the main decoration of the frontal, with hand and machine embroidery to give background texture

Pat Russell and Elizabeth Ward

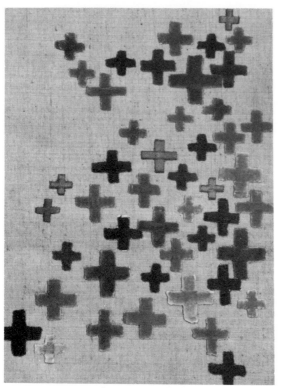

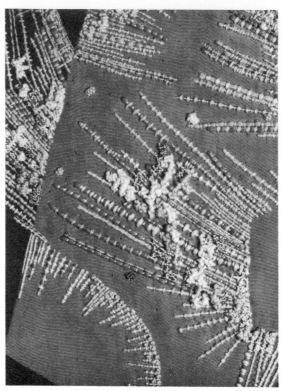

304 *A pulpit fall, consisting of padded velvet crosses in blues, greens and occasionally reds, on a dark purple background. The repetition of a similar shape but with variation in size, is effective. The basic bluish colour scheme is given vitality by the inclusion of red in small crosses. The spacing of the shapes and colour is important* Gillian Hall

305 *Detail of a pulpit fall* Anne Butler

306 '*Burning Bush*'—*a centre piece of an altar frontal* Gloria Cook

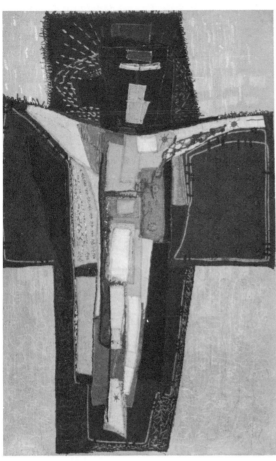

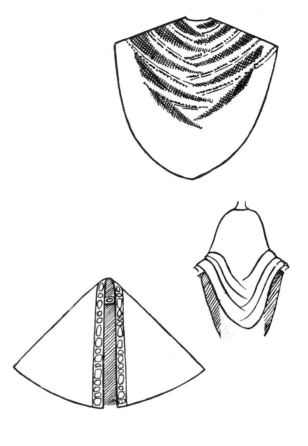

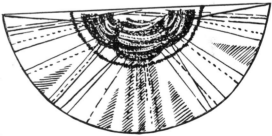

307 A cross. A first experiment in embroidery. A panel in which hand and machine stitchery are combined, the central portion is padded and various materials are used, in yellows, orange, pink, browns and reds. The panel is treated as a sampler, using any materials, and combining any methods of work in order to learn stitchery and to handle fabrics

Edward Holloway

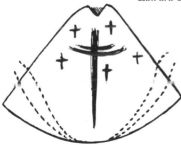

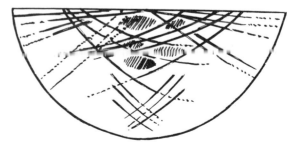

308 Ideas for arrangements of pattern on a chasuble and a cope

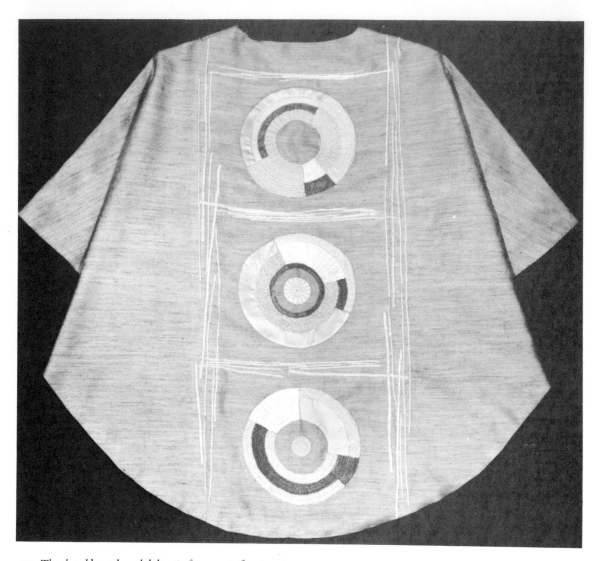

310 *The chasuble, stole and dalmatic from a set of vestments for All Hallows, London Wall, worked on cream fabrics in creams, greys, white and a little gold, mainly in couched threads* Josephine Windebank

(a) Detail from chasuble

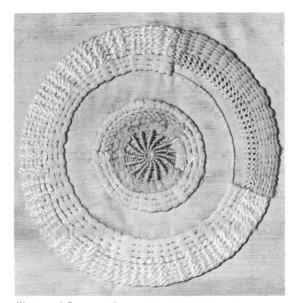

(b) Detail from tunicle

(c) The stole

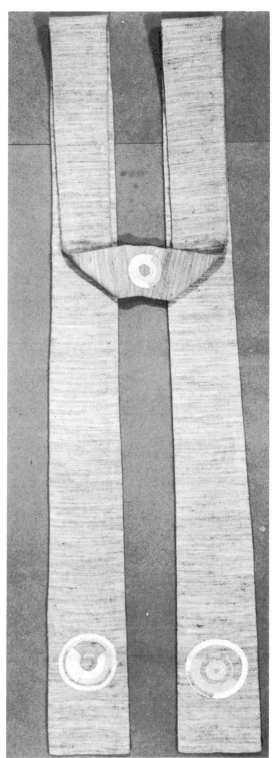

(d) Dalmatic and (e) a detail

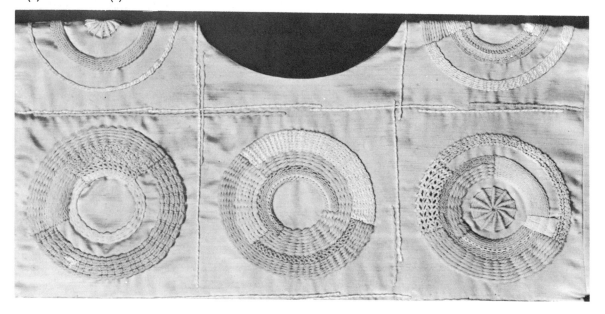

311 Detail of the cross on chasuble. The background is hand printed in pale grey blues in cloud-like shapes. The embroidery is in gold threads, perlita and perle in greys, browns and golds with padded gold kid shapes
Annwyn Morgan

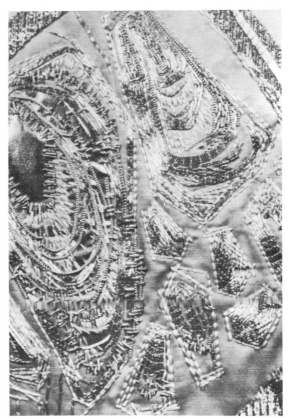

312 Detail from a cope, with embroidery in gold threads, gold kid and khaki satin over padding, on a white ground
Barbara Dawson

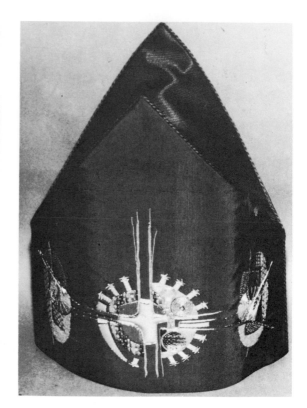

313 *A cope of scarlet cloth, embroidered with a huge sun in pinks, yellows and oranges and a quantity of yellow wooden beads*   Josephine Windebank

314 *A mitre in scarlet corded silk embroidered in gold threads and padded gold kid*   Margaret Nash

(*a*) *Detail from front*

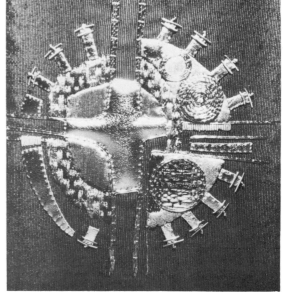

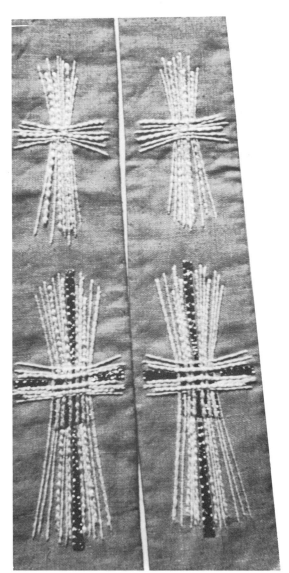

316 *Embroidered ends of stole on white linen. Makerere College, Kampala, Uganda*

315 *The end of a stole showing figures in ordinary day dress. Worked entirely in gold threads* Dorothy Birchmore

(a)

317 (a) *Embroidered ends of stole on white linen*
(b) *A burse to match the stole*

These go with an altar frontal containing a design of a large sun, with African symbols. The original embroidery is in the Makerere College, Kampala, Uganda

(b)

Lettering is a skilful art. It requires a great deal of practice to become proficient but if a good background knowledge is obtained, this is invaluable to anyone who designs for embroidery as there are many occasions when it is required. Here it is briefly touched upon, but this is to give an awareness of its possibilities in design and its contribution to design in embroidery. In order to make further study of lettering a list of books is suggested in the bibliography.

The essential qualities of lettering are that it is legible and at the same time is pleasing to the eye as a pattern. Good spacing and proportion are therefore necessary, in other words good design. Lettering is a matter of sound drawing and a sense of balance of pattern against background. Used alone it may be sufficiently well planned as the sole decoration of banners, for the embellishment of household articles and for dress and accessories. The Roman alphabet on which classical lettering was based is unsuitable with its serifs, for embroidery, but its proportions are beautiful and might be the model from which other letter forms are invented. Calligraphy in which a brush or pen is used freely, possesses a great deal of vitality if drawn with conviction and sensitivity, and is a letter form ideal as a basis for embroidery design. Spacing and layout must be planned with care, the letters should be well constructed and readable and their proportions must suit the whole conception of the decoration if for a banner or frontal.

Single initial letters or monograms for the decoration of sports clothes and household linens do not give the same problems, as if well drawn and designed for the purpose, and within the given area that is sufficient. The placing of the letters on the article or the garment is part of the design but less of a problem than when fitting words together which should be legible and at the same time make good pattern.

In planning a whole piece of lettering for embroidery in which a number of words are used together, there is first of all the problem of what kind of letters to use; whether to keep to capitals, whether to use capitals and uncials or whether to use uncials alone. Another form of lettering altogether might be chosen based on Gill's sans serif, which is a block letter based on the Roman proportions but without serifs and no variation in the thicknesses of the strokes. This form is workable in a number of methods, either in outline or in solid stitchery. Again an italic style might be more suitable than that of upright letters. Several roughs should be attempted before deciding upon the style most suitable for the embroidery in mind. The beginnings and endings of the lines of lettering should make a pleasant pattern as well as that made by the distribution of the letters. Here it must be decided whether the beginning of each row should be level with uneven endings or whether both beginning and ending should be uneven. Roughly cut paper letters if the size warrants this, would help in laying out a design in which large letters are to be used. They may be placed quite unevenly, non parallel to one another and may look better than when spaced conventionally but this cannot be ascertained without trying them out. Most lettering looks thicker and heavier when embroidered, therefore it is better to make it that much finer in the design so that it does not become clumsy.

There are innumerable forms of lettering from which to select styles suitable for adaptation to embroidery, but these forms must be understood before playing around with them as all letters are limited in the alterations they can stand without losing their qualities of legibility. They may be elongated or flattened, made more square or rounder, made thicker or thinner but these variations can only go so far without loss of character.

If more practical information is required by the non-letterer there are good books on the basic principles of lettering, but it is hoped that this very brief account of its creative possibilities as an exciting subject for design will develop an appreciation and eventually help in distinguishing the difference between good and poorly constructed lettering, in becoming aware of good layout as against that without design, and in being able to use it freely interpreted in embroidery for many purposes.

318 *Letters showing different styles and suggestions of ways in which some of these might be embroidered*

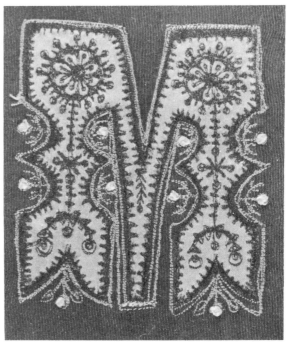

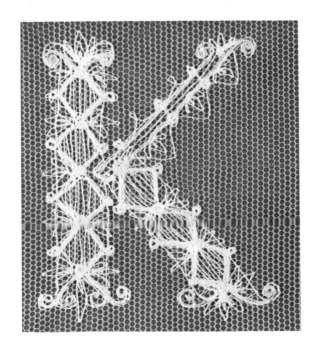

319 The letter 'P' in hand stitchery. Based on the Roman
alphabet
The letter 'K' machine stitched on net
The letter 'M' in appliqué and machine stitchery,
using lurex. These letters are three from a complete
alphabet of all the letters from A–Z each worked
differently and planned to suit a particular type of
work. All designed and worked by Eirian Short

320 'BUS' *lettering in appliqué and stitchery giving an abstract result*   Barbara Dawson

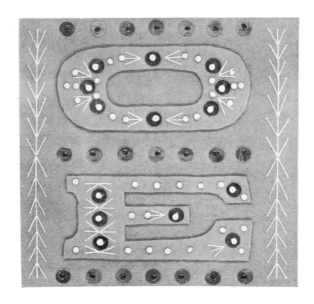

321 Part of a Christmas card. Felt on felt, with simple decoration of beads, sequins and stitchery   Anne Preston

Heraldry cannot be gone into in this book but it plays an important part in embroidery designed for civil and ecclesiastical purposes, for ceremonial robes, banners and decorations for liveried companies and civic centres. Its strict rules must be adhered to, one of the most important being that metal must be used on colour and colour on metal. This immediately limits the use of colour and often the type of design, which was originally invented as symbolism to distinguish the bands of knights during the crusades, when they were otherwise clothed in armour and indistinguishable from one another. The divisions of the field are also rigid, the quarterings and superimposing of symbols within the shield are a test in planning good design which must give clarity at a distance. There are excellent books on heraldry which explain all the rules and with their limitations it is possible to create superb designs. It is a first-class medium for embroidery as it depends for its vitality on well-planned design which is at the same time essentially simple.

322 An heraldic cushion cover designed for Eton College Chapel in cross stitch Constance Howard

Bibliography

Art and Design
Basic Design: The Dynamics of Visual Form   Maurice de Saumarez   Studio Vista
Elements of Design: Donald Anderson Hart   Rinehart and Winston, New York
The Meaning of Art: Herbert Read   Pelican 1949
The Nature of Design: David Pye   Studio Vista
Snow Crystals: W. A. Bentley and W. J. Humphreys   Dover Publications Inc., New York
The Story of Art: E. M. Gombrich   Phaidon Press

Colour
Embroidery and Colour: Constance Howard   Batsford
Handbook of Colour: A. Komerup and S. H. Wanschen   Methuen
Interactions of Colour: Josef Albers   Yale University Press 1963
Fabric Printing by Hand: Stephen Russ   Studio Vista
Tie and Dye as a Present Day Craft: Anne Maile   Mills and Boon
The Use of Vegetable Dyes: V. Thurstan   Dryad Press, Leicester

Embroidery
American Needlework: Rose Wilder Lane   Batsford
The Art of Embroidery: M. Schuette and S. Muller-Christensen   Thames and Hudson
Bead Embroidery: Joan Edwards   Batsford
The Craft of Embroidery: Alison Liley   Mills and Boon
Dictionary of Embroidery Stitches: Mary Thomas   Hodder and Stoughton
Ecclesiastical Embroidery: Beryl Dean   Batsford
Embroidery Stitches: Barbara Snook   Batsford
Hungarian Peasant Embroidery: Edit Fél   Batsford
Linen Embroidery: Etta Campbell   Batsford
Machine Embroidery: Jennifer Gray   Batsford
Machine Embroidery: Christine Risley   Mills and Boon
Patchwork: Averil Colby   Batsford
Patchwork Quilts: Averil Colby   Batsford
Samplers: Averil Colby   Batsford
Swedish Embroidery: Eivor Fisher   Batsford
Needlemade Rugs: Sybil Matthews   Mills and Boon
Colour and Texture in Creative Textile Craft: Rolf Hartung   Batsford
Creative Textile Craft: Thread and Fabric: Rolf Hartung   Batsford
Art of Cutwork and Appliqué: Herta Puls   Batsford
The Seminole Patchwork Book: Cheryl Bradkin   Yours Truly Publication Inc
The Batsford Book of Canvas Work: Mary Rhodes   Batsford
The Batsford Encyclopaedia of Embroidery Stitches: Anne Butler   Batsford
The Batsford Encyclopaedia of Embroidery Techniques: Gay Swift   Batsford
Embroidery in Religion and Ceremonial: Beryl Dean   Batsford

Embroidery *continued*
Design in Embroidery: Kathleen Whyte   Batsford
Needleweaving: Edith John   Batsford
Experimental Embroidery: Edith John   Batsford
Machine Stitches: Anne Butler   Batsford
Quilting: Averil Colby   Batsford
Creative Thread Design: Nair Morris   Batsford
Metal Thread Embroidery: Barbara Dawson   Batsford
Quilting: Technique, Design and Application: Eirian Short   Batsford

Folk Art
African Design: Margaret Trowell   Faber and Faber 1960
Benin Art: Forman and Dach   Paul Hamlyn
Exotic Art: Forman   Spring Books
Folk Art in Pictures: Karel Sourek   Spring Books
Indian Art of Central America: F. J. Dockstader   Cory, Adams and MacKay, Limited
Indigo Blue Print in Slovac Folk Art: J. Vydra   Artea Prague 1954
Klee: Translated by Stuart Hord   Thames and Hudson
Primitive Art: Christensen   Bonanza Books, New York
The Scythians: Tamara Talbot Rice   Thames and Hudson

Lettering
Calligraphy Today: Heather Child   Studio Vista
Lettering Today: John Brinkley   Studio Vista
Love and Joy about Letters: Ben Shahn   Cory, Adams and MacKay
Lettering Techniques: John Lancaster   Batsford

Natural Form
Form in Art and Nature: (Kunst und Natur Form)   Georg Schmidt   Basilius Press, Basel
Forms and Pattern in Nature: Wolf Strache   Peter Owen
Life under the Sea: Maurice Buston   Spring Books
'Nature et Beauté' series: e.g. *Beautés du Monde Invisible*   Larousse
Spectacles de la Nature: Larousse
Splendour in Nature and any in this series e.g. *Minerals and Rocks*   H. W. Ball   Rathbone Books
'Nature et Beauté' series e.g. *Beautés du Monde Invisible*   Larousse
'Symbol' series Prentice Hall International, London

> *Evolution:* Jean Rostand
> *Time:* Le Lionnais
> *The Sun:* Etienne Lalon
> *The Sky:* Jean-Claude Pecker
> *The Written Word:* Etiemble
> *Volcanoes:* Haroun Tazieff

Symbolism
The Book of Signs: Rudolf Koch   Dover Publications Inc., New York

Suppliers

Great Britain

*Embroidery threads and
accessories. Many stock
fabrics, beads and sequins,
and gold and silver kid as well*

Mrs Mary Allen
Wirksworth, Turnditch,
Derbyshire DE4 4BN

Art Needlework Industries
7 St Michael's Mansions
Ship Street
Oxford OX1 3DG

Brodwaith Embroidery
5 Lion Yard
Dolgellau
Gwynedd LL40 1DG

The Campden Needlecraft
  Centre
High Street
Chipping Campden
Gloucestershire

Craftsman's Mark Limited
Broadlands, Shortheath
Farnham, Surrey

The Danish House
16 Sloane Street
London SW1X 9NB

de Denne Limited
159/161 Kenton Road
Kenton, Harrow
Middlesex HA3 0EU

B Francis
4 Glenworth Street
London NW1

William Hall & Co Ltd
177 Stanley Road
Cheadle Hulme
Cheadle, Cheshire
SK8 6RF

The Handicraft Shop
5 Oxford Road
Altrincham, Cheshire

Handweavers Studio
29 Haroldstone Road
Walthamstow
London E17 7AN

The Handworkers' Market
6 Bull Street, Holt,
Norfolk NR25 6HP

Harrods Limited
London W1

Mace and Nairn
89 Crane Street
Salisbury, Wiltshire SP1 2PY

MacCulloch and Wallis
25–26 Dering Street
London W1R 0BH

Needle Art House
Albion Mills
Westgate, Wakefield
West Yorkshire WF2 9SG

The Nimble Thimble
26 The Green
Bilton, Rugby CV22 7LY

Richmond Art and Craft
Dept E1, 181 City Road
Cardiff CF2 3JB

Christine Riley
53 Barclay Street
Stonehaven
Kincardineshire AB3 2AR

Royal School of Needlework
25 Princes Gate
Kensington SW7 1QE

Stephen Simpson Ltd
Avenham Road Works
Preston, Lancashire

The Silver Thimble
33 Gay Street
Bath

Spinning Jenny
Bradley, Keighley
West Yorkshire BD20 9DD

J Henry Smith Limited
Park Road, Calverton
Woodborough
nr Nottingham

Teazle Embroidery
35 Boothferry Road
Hull, HU3 6UA

Texere Yarns
9 Peckover Street
Bradford
West Yorkshire BD1 5BD

Elizabeth Tracy
45 High Street
Haslemere, Surrey

Beads and sequins
Sesame Ventures
Greenham Hall
Wellington, Somerset

Ells and Farrier Ltd
5 Princes Street
London W1R 8PH

All materials for design
George Rowney and Co Ltd
10 Percy Street
London W1

Winsor and Newton Ltd
51–52 Rathbone Place
London W1P 1AB

Coloured and tissue papers
Paperchase
216 Tottenham Court Road
London W1

F G Kettle
127 High Holborn
London WC1

United States of America
Embroidery threads and accessories

Appleton Brothers of London
West Main Road
Little Compton
Rhode Island 02837

American Crewel Studio
Box 553 Westfield
New Jersey 07091

American Thread
   Corporation
90 Park Avenue
New York

Casa de las Tejedoras
1618 East Edinger
Santa Ana
California 92705

Colonial Textiles
2604 Cranbrook
Ann Arbor
Michigan 48104

Craft Kaleidoscope
6412 Ferguson Street
Indianapolis 46220

Dharma Trading Company
1952 University Avenue
Berkeley
California 94704

Folklorico Yarn Co
522 Ramona Street
Palo Alto 94301
California

The Golden Eye
Box 205
Chestnut Hill
Massachusetts 02167

Heads and Tails
River Forest
Illinois 60305

The Needle's Point Studio
216 Appleblossom Court
Vienna, Virginia 22180

Sutton Yarns
2054 Yonge Street
Toronto 315
Ontario, Canada

Threadbenders
2260 Como Avenue
St Paul, Minnesota 55108

The Thread Shed
307 Freeport Road
Pittsburgh
Pennsylvania 15215

David Traum Inc
West Paterson
New Jersey 07424

Yarn Bazaar
Yarncrafts Limited
3146 M Street
North West Washington DC

Leather, gold and silver kid
Aerolyn Fabrics Inc
380 Broadway, New York

All materials for design
Winsor and Newton Inc
881 Broadway, New York
and
55 Winsor Drive
Secaucus, New Jersey 07094

Index